Stephen Gard

Nasty Noises

Stephen Gard

Nasty Noises

Error as a Compositional Element in Electro-Acoustic Music

VDM Verlag Dr. Müller

Imprint

Bibliographic information by the German National Library: The German National Library lists this publication at the German National Bibliography; detailed bibliographic information is available on the Internet at http://dnb.d-nb.de.

Any brand names and product names mentioned in this book are subject to trademark, brand or patent protection and are trademarks or registered trademarks of their respective holders. The use of brand names, product names, common names, trade names, product descriptions etc. even without a particular marking in this works is in no way to be construed to mean that such names may be regarded as unrestricted in respect of trademark and brand protection legislation and could thus be used by anyone.

Cover image: www.purestockx.com

Publisher:
VDM Verlag Dr. Müller Aktiengesellschaft & Co. KG , Dudweiler Landstr. 125 a, 66123 Saarbrücken, Germany,
Phone +49 681 9100-698, Fax +49 681 9100-988,
Email: info@vdm-verlag.de

Zugl.: Sydney, University of Sydney, Diss., 2006

Copyright © 2008 VDM Verlag Dr. Müller Aktiengesellschaft & Co. KG and licensors
All rights reserved. Saarbrücken 2008

Produced in USA and UK by:
Lightning Source Inc., La Vergne, Tennessee, USA
Lightning Source UK Ltd., Milton Keynes, UK
BookSurge LLC, 5341 Dorchester Road, Suite 16, North Charleston, SC 29418, USA

ISBN: 978-3-8364-9352-9

CONTENTS

CHAPTER 1: INTRODUCTION 5

1.0 Nasty Noises 5
1.1 Glitch Music 5
1.2 The Tradition of Shock and Confrontation in Art 6
1.3 Duchamp and the 'readymade' 7
1.4 Scope of this Work 7

CHAPTER 2: SEARCHING THE LITERATURE 8

2.0 Search Terms 8
2.1 Material in the Dissertation Abstracts Database 9
2.2 Other Voices 11
2.3 On the Topic of 'Wrongness' in Music 11
2.4 Inclusion and Exclusion of Noise as Musical Material 13
2.5 On the Nature of 'Glitch' Music 14
2.6 On the Topic of Recontextualizing Sound 17
2.7 On the Blurring of Boundaries between Art and Pop Musics 20
2.8 Conclusion 21

CHAPTER 3: DEFINITIONS AND DERIVATIONS 22

3.0 Defining and Exampling Some Terms 22
3.1 'Nasty' Noises 22
3.2 Glitch Music 23
3.3 Microsound 24
3.4 Noise Music 25
3.5 lowercase music 25
3.6 Techno 25
3.7 Sampling 26
3.8 Turntablism 27
3.9 Recontextualization 28

CHAPTER 4: GLITCH AND GLITCHING 30

4.0 Why Is Glitch Music? 30

4.1 The Never Ending Story 30

4.2 Do It Yourself 30

4.3 Error = Individuality 30

4.4 Refracted Meanings 31

4.5 On Deconstruction 32

4.6 The Decay of Composition 32

4.7 Blitz 33

4.8 Glitz 33

4.9 Sitz 34

4.10 Intertextuality, and the Anxiety of Influence 34

4.11 Glitchers on Glitching 36

4.12 My Glitch 36

4.13 *Spirit Trace* 38

4.14 *Study 1.0 (FM)* 38

4.15 *Village Football* 39

4.16 *BAG* 39

4.17 Talking the Talk: Modex 40

4.18 Walking the Walk: Plex 41

CHAPTER FIVE: THE ART OF GLITCH 43

5.0 Grabbing Glitch 43

5.1 The Limits of Glitch 43

5.2 Neuter Noises 45

APPENDIX: 'CARRIERS', AN ESSAY IN RADIOSONIC GLITCH 47

REFERENCES 51

Books 51

Articles in Journals, Magazines and Newspapers 52

Internet Material 54

Other Internet Material 55

ACKNOWLEDGEMENT
Thanks to my colleague Amanda Cole,
for drawing my attention to the glitch in my music.

CHAPTER 1: INTRODUCTION

1.0 Nasty Noises

A couple of years ago, a well-known Australian chamber ensemble was being interviewed on ABC-FM radio, concerning their current national tour. The interviewer asked if the ensemble played much contemporary music, and if their audiences enjoyed it. There was a pause. 'You mean, do we play Nasty Noises?' asked one musician. Everyone laughed.

Everyone near the microphone laughed, that is. The quantity of listeners that laughed was not reported, but the musician went on to say that many of their audiences still preferred familiar nineteenth century pieces. Such audiences often received performances of 'modern' works with distaste, even vexation, she remarked.

That 'modern' music sounds to some ears like 'nasty noises' is not news. Violent audience reaction against first performances of Stravinksy's *Rite of Spring* and of Schoenberg's *Verklärte Nacht* are now part of musical folklore (McLeish, 1978; McDonald, 1987). Audience vexation, and critical fury at 'new' music goes back several centuries (Slonimsky, 1978). Fear, and rage, are familiar responses to the new and the different,[1] and a listener's anger at performances of 'modern' music may arise from simple alarm in the presence of a phenomenon beyond immediate comprehension, or from an implied challenge to the authority of her or his learning. Offences against the unaccustomed ear - dissonance, formlessness, the disturbing orchestral timbres of 'extended technique' - can seem to deliberately flout received modes of practice and appreciation; they may appear to negate all that the perceiver understands and values. To such a listener, an arts practice that includes the disjunct and the unpleasant must seem wilfully perverse. Can the repellent, the erroneous, amount to an artistic elemental? Has it already? In a postmodern age, the answer is 'yes', however, a question is raised. Can these toxins retain their intended irritant potency when assimilated? Do nasty noises stay nasty if they become familiar?

1.1 Glitch Music

The art-form here to inspected is *glitch music,* an electroacoustic sub-genre that has attracted attention over the past five years, not least because a weighty polemic has been constructed around it. The idea is simple: glitch music is straightforward electroacoustic music constructed from sonorities signifying error, especially the sounds produced by

---

[1] 'We fear things in proportion to our ignorance of them.' Titus Livius (54 BCE – 17 CD).

malfunctioning devices, or corrupted files. In the world of dance music, where novelty fuels the creative boiler, glitch can take the place of a percussion instrument; for example, the static produced by a voltage spike might substitute for a cymbal crash. In the stochastic realm of electronic Art Music, where an obvious pulse is often (but not always) scorned, glitch might appear as gesture, texture, or timbre.

Noise – any non-traditional timbre – has been imported into music for over a century, if we choose as a starting point the cannon blasts in Tchaikovsky's *1812, Ouverture Solonelle* op. 49, but glitch is the music of *angst*, not celebration. Contemporary writers discussing glitch music assert so many claims for its significance that a disinterested investigator might wonder if they protest too much, if there is not a hint of hysteria in such querulous voices. Are error, irony, antithesis, evaporating into aesthetic despair? When it comes time to annotate this era of Art, will glitch be dubbed the glorious sunset of electronic music?

1.2 The Tradition of Shock and Confrontation in Art

Modernism, as an artistic movement, has aimed to confront, shock, or at least surprise its audience (Read, 1959, p. 287; Machlis, 1963, p. 315; Croft 1988, pp. 409-429). Its weapon is novelty, its target the urban and the industrial. Its intent is purgative, cathartic, revisionist and radical, in a word, 'progressive'. That the works of *echt* musical Modernists like Schoenberg and Webern, (first reviled as nihilists, later recognised as conscientious and pioneering craftsman) can vex audiences nearly a century after their composition, suggests that the radical agenda of Modernism remains unachieved.

Yet, periodising of artistic movements is always dangerous: even Mozart and Haydn sought to destabilise the laws of High Classicism with asymmetries in their phrasings (Machlis, 1961, p. 16). Twentieth century musical Modernism, however, is less prone to charm with such *galant* playfulness than to alarm with disorientation, a legacy of post-WWI cynicism and the youthfulness of Modernism's early practitioners and polemicists.[1] From the late nineteenth century, the proportion of extra-musical reference in composition starts to swell, and the purpose of 'noise' shifts from peripheral and colouristic to the centre of the rhetoric, and we arrive at Gustav Mahler's dictum 'A symphony should be a world', and the planned *Universe Symphony* of Charles Ives. Luigi Russolo, with his 'barkers' and 'clappers', Edgard Varèse and his siren, William Russell with brake-drum, suitcase and firecrackers, all these wait in the wings, along with Percy Grainger and his 'glide' music.

---

[1] See the definition of 'Modernism' in Paul Griffiths, *Encyclopaedia of 20th Century Music*. London: Thames and Hudson, 1992 edition.

1.3 Duchamp and the 'readymade'

Once the principle of 'anything goes' is established in music, we are in the junkyard gallery of Marcel Duchamp, whose Dada art has confounded or delighted critics and audiences since his first New York exhibition of 1915. Duchamp's 'readymades' were art-object as interrogation - a bicycle wheel, a urinal, the Mona Lisa with a moustache, a vapid landscape with two enigmatic drips of colour - such works were simultaneously exhibit and enquiry, insisted Duchamp. Is this junk also Art? So what, then, is Art? Duchamp was violently opposed to the Romantic notion of the individual 'great painter', and he rejected what he termed 'retinal art', representational art, works created merely for looking at; by the age of twenty-five, Duchamp had ceased producing artworks and become chiefly a theorist.[1]

Duchamp's point about the recontextualization of an object, the transubstantiation of junk in a tip to art in a gallery, remains potent, or at least influential. If the familiar and invigorating clamour of steam locomotives working can be arranged into a narrative sequence, labelled *musique concrète*, and become a High Modernist image of urban ruckus, then the small and terrifying clicking of a disc-drive failing can signify the death of electronic music by *glitch*. Not a failure of this music's means, but a failure of the limits of the music's vigour as a representational and even expressive device; a reduction of phenomena to their dusts. In time, the sounds may suggest nothing, not even themselves. As signifiers, they will inscribe silence on silence, in silence. Not with a bang, but with a whisper.

1.4 Scope of this Work

Chapter 2 examines what has recently been written on the subject of glitch in compositional contexts. Chapter 3 defines some terms that will recur. Chapter 4 surveys the work of some glitch composers, their techniques, and their theoretical and aesthetic standpoint. Chapter 5 suggests the significance of glitch for composers of electronic art music now, and perhaps tomorrow.

---

[1] "Duchamp introduced in his work a dimension of irony, almost a mockery of painting itself... that undermined his own belief in painting... What he lacked was faith in art itself, and he sought to replace aesthetic values in his new world with an aggressive intellectualism opposed to the so-called commonsense world." The artist stripped bare by his own theorising, even? From the article 'Marcel Duchamp' by Robert Lebel in the *Encyclopaedia Britannica*, (15th Edition). Lebel was crony, biographer, and critic of Duchamp.

CHAPTER 2: SEARCHING THE LITERATURE

> '[I]n art, a school once established normally deteriorates as it goes on. It achieves perfection in its kind with a startling burst of energy, a gesture too quick for the historian's eye to follow... the equilibrium of the aesthetic life is permanently unstable.' (Collingwood, cited in Read, 1959, p. 11).

2.0 Search Terms

The first difficulty that arose when researching this topic, was that the phenomenon of *glitch music* seemed either too young, too ephemeral, or too eclectic, to have gathered to itself a defining label. A useful catch-all was 'electronica', but it was necessary also to seek writings that mentioned 'clicks 'n' cuts', 'laptop', 'hiphop', 'techno', 'drum and bass', 'jungle', 'microsound', 'house', 'dub', and sub-genres of all these, e.g. 'click-house', or 'industrial-techno' (Monroe, 2003, p. 63), 'dub-reggae', or 'trip-hop' (di Perna, 1998, p. 55), 'Ambient', or 'Gabba' (Barr, 2000, p. I).

In searching databases of scholarly (and other) writings, the keywords 'noise', 'error', 'wrong', 'mistake', 'glitch', and 'unfamiliar' were used, all these in conjunction with 'music' and 'composition', 'composing', or 'compose'. These results were then refined by using the limiting terms 'computer', 'electronic' and 'electroacoustic'. The string *musique concrète* produced a few results. 'Chaos' was also useful, in an unexpected way. These terms were sought among article and book titles, and within the text of abstracts or content summaries.

A great deal of information concerning this area of inquiry is on the Internet. Much of this material consists of comment and opinion, reviews, interviews, record liner notes and other material not necessarily objective in its viewpoint.

However, web-based documents were useful in refining and/or extending search terms. The label 'post-digital music' quickly emerged (Cascone, 2002), as did IDM, Intelligent Dance Music (Sherburne, 2002), and 'microsound' (Roads, 2001). Late in the preparation of the document, 'mash-up' jumped out from cyberspace. Web-searching also helped with tracking the evolution of genres of electronic music, and in obtaining material which was out of print, or which for other reasons was not readily available in any library. Finally, Kim Cascone asserts that glitch music is a phenomenon, even a child of, the Internet; to look elsewhere would be almost to overlook glitch altogether (Cascone, 2000, p. 12).

2.1 Material in the Dissertation Abstracts Database

First task was to see what theses had been written on this topic. There was none addressed specifically to the issue of composing with 'noise'.[1] There were, however, several dissertations which contributed material on associated subjects; extracts from their abstracts below are followed by a comment showing how the thesis content relates to this enquiry.

Steven George Jones examines '… the effect the musical equipment industry may be having on musical creativity by restricting the number of decisions available to the user of electronic musical equipment' (Jones, 1987). If this is the case, are electronic music composers therefore seeking new sounds because the palette of sonorities (synthesizer voices and pre-set audio filters, for example) commercially available to them is too limited or clichéd?

Mark Zaki: 'The emergence of music specifically designed for recording (i.e. computer music) alters the nature of performance. This suggests a shift from expressive artefacts being a spontaneous expression on the part of a performer to a calculated type of affective device created by a composer' (Zaki, 1997). If composers are indeed seeking more 'calculated affective devices', it may explain the inclusion of 'nasty noises' in many present musics.

Richard Schmidt James: '… some of the impetus behind early efforts in electronic music had been at work for decades: interest in noise composition, scientific construction of new sounds, and freedom from the influence and limitations of the human performer. Even some of the techniques central to electronic music had already been explored and applied in rudimentary fashion in film music, noise composition, and early electronic instruments.' (James, 1981). James's study contributes to our search for a history of including 'noise' in electronic music.

Michael Edward Von Der Linn: 'Degeneracy [*Entartung*] was attributed [by social critics] to the negative physical and psychological effects of modern industrialized society on the individual. Exposure to urban noise and pollution, for example, was linked to nervousness. Critics argued that modernity was having a similar effect on contemporary music' (Von Der Linn, 1999). Here is more evidence for the historical inclusion of 'noise'. (See Chapter 2.6 *re* the ideas of Luigi Russulo.)

---

[1] David Bracket (Bracket, 2002, p. 224) remarks on the difficulty of including late-twentieth-century music in the 'canon of acceptable musicology dissertation topics'.

Christoph Both: 'Not only did concepts of information theory initiate a compositional shift from model-based to process-oriented design in the works of both Hiller and Stockhausen, they also had a considerable historical impact. Simultaneously they gave birth to computer music in America and initiated the decay of serialism in Europe in the 1950s' (Both, 1995). 'Process-oriented' means that the sounds suggested their own implementation, a compositional practice used and discussed by Pierre Schaeffer (see Chapter 5.0).

Kenneth Igarashi: 'Noise... improv... was a musical style which developed in the late 1970s and early 1980s in New York City and the San Francisco Bay Area... in its emphasis on multiplicity, spontaneity, fragmentation and individuality; its employment of an eclectic sonic vocabulary which incongruously juxtaposes borrowed elements; and its challenge of originality and a single compositional voice, it is readily comprehended as a post-modern phenomenon' (Igarashi, 1997). Igarashi's study adds more to the history of noise composition; it also highlights the 'live' and 'improv' (improvisation) components of the ensuing genres.

William Ganse Little offers a literary-critical perspective, examining: '... the philosophic, social, and aesthetic implications of twentieth-century America's obsession with eliminating waste... the American consumer culture fetishizes waste as a toxic other whose proper treatment delivers the individual subject from the wasteland of modern life' (Little, 1998). Hence, the 're-use' of vinyl recordings (see 'turntablism' in Chapter 3.8) negates their 'trashy' messages? Or somehow justifies their continuing presence, their occupation of physical and cognitive space, by assigning them a more useful and meaningful rôle in today's complex society? Recontextualising system noise somehow 'cleanses' it?

Brett Foster James: 'Heidegger... warned humankind about the dangers of being 'Enframed' by technology - that is, made a mere resource or cog for the technological process. Heidegger argues that humankind is either Enframed by technology, or is living at peace with it, in a state of poiesis' (James, 1995). Thus, machine noises (for example) are being incorporated in music to avoid this 'enframement'. The artist is 'fighting back' against technology, on our behalf. *Poiesis* means 'productivity', 'creativity', as opposed (in this context) to passive acceptance.

David Kahn Feurzeig: '[Thelonious] Monk was long held to have inadequate piano technique. Defences of his playing have not confronted the disturbing peculiarities of his music... an analysis of his 1968 recording of "Round midnight' shows that its most awkward moments are manifestations of tricksterism, not flaws' (Feurzeig, 1997). Jazz composer Thelonious Monk using error as a compositional element? The Trickster is a folkloric figure who '... exposes norms, ideology and categorization as static and therefore flawed human constructs' (Gates, 1988, p. 6). Are error and 'noise' then, tricks for levering contemporary music out of stasis?[1]

2.2 Other Voices

Other associated writings were located using a variety of sources; *Répertoire International de Littérature Musicale* (RILM), Music Index, on-line library catalogues, library shelf-browsing, the bibliographies of the writings themselves, CD inserts, concert programs, word-of-mouth, and other media. These are identified and annotated below according to their relevance to this short enquiry.

2.3 On the Topic of 'Wrongness' in Music

'Wrongness' in music may be defined here as material that a *listener* identifies as not belonging to the text of a work being heard. This includes *errors of execution*, e.g. incorrect fingerings, poor intonation, over-blowing, that result in a variant realisation of a score, and *misreadings*, where a work is misrepresented due to inaccurate score-decoding, e.g. forgetting the key signature, miscounting rests, or misunderstanding some instruction. Wrongness is easier to detect in a familiar work: it amounts to a misquotation, such as, *Shall I compare thee to a summer's eve? Thou art more lively and more tempting.* Or perhaps:

Figure 1 Mozart K. 545

Wrongness is also easier to detect, or at any rate, to label as such, in an unfamiliar work which has a tonal centre. Here, any intended dissonance has a brief, colouristic role, and

---

[1] See also Thomas M. Maier, ' 'Error is an excellent thing': Analysis and interpretation of 'errors' in some of John Cage's compositions from the late 1940s'. *Archiv für Musikwissenschaft* Vol. 58, Issue 2 (2001): 131-143. Maier speaks of '… Cage's special pleasure in installing small, nearly imperceptible mistakes in the 'micro-macrocosmic' plans underlying his compositions [which] 'heal' the composition from a pure and one-sided rationality.' (Abstract text.)

must quickly be resolved, for example, to the home or a related key.[1] Otherwise, the 'rules' of Common Practice music, as formulated by Rameau, forbid such excursions.[2]

A tradition of centuries of such tonal music had educated the ears of the first critics who encountered twentieth century music. To most of these listeners, new works contained errors; sometimes the music seemed to consist of nothing else. Frederick Corder's 'On the Cult of Wrong Notes' (Corder, 1915) has become a cult classic of reactionary music criticism. Strauss, asserted Corder, had 'no ear', Scriabine (*sic*) was a 'lunatic', Schoenberg an 'idiot', and Bartók's work, 'mere ordure'. Corder's article, however, was prophetic in two senses. Firstly, he notes his being dismissed as an 'academic' for his unpopular views of modern music; secondly, he refutes the contemporaneous opinion that '... art has said its last word and that chaos must supersede...' Can postmodernism thus be only a latter-day phenomenon? Lyotard suggests that every age has its postmodernist phase (Lyotard, 1984). Corder may have been observing such a phase-shift of cultures taking place in his own era.

Wrongness, however, can make sometimes 'make itself at home'. Bruno H. Repp (Repp, 1996) claims that a typical concert audience is unlikely to notice more than a fraction of a pianist's inaccuracies, due to the contextual 'fit' of most mistakes. Thus, 'error' is error only until it becomes assimilated into the culture of a work, which is possible due to the human mind's tendency to categorise the unfamiliar, making order from chaos.[3] James R. Hamilton (Hamilton, 1999) lists some artefacts of live performance (breath noises, creaking chairs, instrument key clicks) and asks, if these 'errors' are a concomitant of music performance, can they truly be dismissed as 'noise'? Thomas Kupper asks a similar question, in the context of 'perfect' digital recordings: does such perfection remove authenticity? (Kupper, 2002). Wrongness may have a motivation: Reinhold Friedl asserts that the purpose of contemporary music is to cause performers and audience alike physical and emotional pain, and that this arises from composers' sadomasochistic impulses (Friedl, 2003).

---

[1] But c.f. Brian Heyer 'Liszt... was perhaps the first composer... to create music with a conscious awareness of [tonality], and it was not until Schoenberg that it assumed crucial historical significance. Almost all the tonal music written during the three previous centuries emerged without reference, tacit or otherwise, to the concept now thought to define its essential condition.' (Hyer, 2004).

[2] Jean-Phillip Rameau *Traité de L'Harmonie Reduite a ses Principes Naturels*, (1722)

[3] A seminal paper (1949) on human cognition and perception included this axiom: '... directive processes in the organism operate to organize the perceptual field in such a way as to maximize percepts relevant to current needs.' Bruner, Jerome S. and Postman, Leo. (1949). 'On the Perception of Incongruity: A Paradigm.' *Journal of Personality*, 18: 206-223.

'Wrongness' in music, then, falls into two classes: *error*, and the *unfamiliar*. What is unfamiliar is often affronting, even threatening, and the most affronting of new music has often been labelled *noise*.

2.4 Inclusion and Exclusion of Noise as Musical Material

'A weed is a plant growing in the wrong place.'[1]

The word 'noise' itself derives ultimately from the Latin word *nausea*. Noise is often defined as any 'unpleasant' sound, and this implies more than aesthetic distaste, suggesting even that noise is a health hazard. The ancients disallowed the interval of a tritone in their music, calling it *diabolus in musica,* widening that interval during performance to achieve consonance (Bent, 2004). Monteverdi was the first to include the dominant seventh in his harmonic textures as a destabilizer and lever towards other tonalities (Hyer, 2004). The *appoggiatura* became a favourite Baroque non-harmonic ornament, as did the *acciaccatura*, adding piquancy to a melody by briefly swerving from and deforming it. *Acciaccatura* means (roughly) 'crushing', a technique not-unknown in the preparation of 'glitch' sonic materials. J.S. Bach used dissonant (diminished and augmented) intervals as strong modulatory catalysts.

These few examples suggest an historical progression in the tolerance of 'inadmissible' material into musical texts, which finally arrives at the use of 'clusters', clots of pitches, often percussive, first used in the early 20th century by Cowell and Bartók, and as the *Grove Dictionary of Music and Musicians* remarks 'commonplace since the 1950s'.

Noise began to find a role in music after the latter half of the nineteenth century: the eighteen anvils Wagner calls for in *Das Rheingold* (f.p. 1869), the cannon and church-bells in Tchaikovsky's *1812, Ouverture Solonelle op. 49* (f.p. 1882), and the cowbells of Mahler's *Sixth Symphony* (f.p. 1903). Each is an identifiable sound from the world 'outside' music, bearing with it a passport of references that permit its residence in programmatic works like these.

Such upheavals move the boundaries of the permissible; listening ears are re-educated. To shift the focus to a contemporary context: Sergio Friere gives an historical account of the loudspeaker as 'mediator' between listener and music, and claims that currently, listeners to

---

[1] Variously attributed.

electronic media must participate more actively in 'the definition of their object of contemplation' (Friere, 2003, p. 70). Listeners in the past may have attended 'beyond' the surface noise of a recording to the music behind it, but the surface noise is now 'admitted', heard as part of the performance. Guy-Marc Hinant's 'TOHU BOHU' (Hinant, 2003) uses a 'noisy' prose style to discuss the evolution of noise and not-noise in music. Hinant's article is granulated into 78 seemingly disparate 'fragments' whose coherence becomes apparent only after the entire text is read, a demonstration of 'medium as message': it is visual microsound.

As for sounds that come with a 'passport', Holger Schultze writes, 'Aleatoric games are a way to make room for emerging intentions… we arrive somewhere on the other side of the boundaries, which we had not even recognized as such' (Schultze, 2003). Thus, composers employing 'glitch' may seek to avoid familiar figures of musical rhetoric by intruding textural and gestural elements that bring no 'luggage' with them; noises so 'foreign' that they have no meaning save as pure sonic events.

Finally, Peter Shapiro, explaining *turnablism* to readers of *The Wire*, examined the work of several sound-artists, including 'spin doctor' Christian Marclay, whose abuse of vinyl records is intended 'to intervene in consumerism's cult of the object… [b]y foregrounding surface noise' (Shapiro, 1999, p. 43). That is, a vinyl recording is itself a musical performance, and so must include the scratches on its surfaces. Marclay (and others) politicise the act of listening by a deconstructive reading of the experience. Glitch (here, surface noise) destabilises the authority of the record as a definitive text, and thereby challenges the capitalist economy that tries to control musical expression *via* the creation and commodification of recorded music, its reduction to a mere object. In the language of commerce, music as a *good*.

2.5 On the Nature of 'Glitch' Music

What is 'glitch' music, and what is its genesis? Strictly speaking, a 'glitch' is a sudden and considerable change in voltage, a 'spike' in an electrical circuit, likely to cause component damage and/or malfunction. *Glitsch* is Yiddish for 'slide' (from German *gleiten*, glide, slide, slip), in the sense of 'slipping out of control'; *glitch* probably entered the mainstream English language in the early Sixties, as a result of the massive publicity accompanying the United States' space program, where a glitch in a launching or other electrical system was a serious matter.[1] Most recently, the word has applied to digital environments, and refers to artefacts of the functioning of such equipment, or flaws in the substance of storage media that cause errors in the reproduction of data, and the sonic substances ('nasty noises') resulting from these circumstances, employable as compositional material in electroacoustic works.

How long has this been going on in digital music? Yasunao Tone writes of performing his 'damaged CD' music in 1986, in the presence of John Cage, who 'laughed loudly', and shook his (Tone's) hand (Tone, 2003, p. 13), but Tone's experiments had started in 1984, when CD technology became available to the consumer (Stuart, 2003, p. 48). Caleb Stuart comments that the sound of a CD 'skipping' due to dust or scratches on its surface is a 'common experience of any café-goer', one that stops their conversation (Stuart, 2003, p. 47). 'Recognition' of nasty noises may precede their being tamed: the café audience may come to consider a skipping CD as part of the background music, and rather than stopping their conversation, may perhaps call for it to be played again, even for the machine to be set on 'Repeat Play'.

Emmanuelle Loubet documented an 'explosion' of Japanese digital performers in the 1990s, most with no musical training, chiefly interested in manipulating (that is, misusing) digital sound and other computer files, for example, text or graphical data (Loubet, 2000). These somewhat nihilistic laptop performers incorporated any musical genre and/or sound-making device into their work. All such 'imported' cultural commodities are considered by Japanese artists to possess equal cultural value, claims Loubet, and materials can be 'plundered' without any need to reconcile conflicting cultural texts. 'Glitch' in this context means both 'misread' files, e.g. image files realised as sounds, as well as the juxtaposition of sharply unrelated musics. Loubet observes that the work of these young artists consciously attacks the tenets of Japanese education, which emphasises rote learning, and discourages enquiry or criticism. Thus, Sachiko M. created 'anti-private' or 'anti-memory' music to oppose her society's preference for rote learning, and its commercialisation of culture.

---

[1] Jonathon Green *Bloomsbury Dictionary of New Words*. (1991), though Green does not provide a citation to support his claim of first recorded usage being 1962. *The Macquarie Dictionary* (1990) gives a 1982 citation for *glitch* in a computer software review. (The Macquarie suggests a derivation from 'glitter' or 'gleam'). Interestingly, the 1997 edition of *The Oxford Dictionary of New Words* does not list *glitch*, though it claims to cover words that have been 'in the news' in the mid-nineties. Wikipedia (http://en.wikipedia.org/wiki/Glitch and http://en.wikipedia.org/wiki/Glitch_%28music%29) notes the usage of 'glitch' in digital logic-circuit engineering jargon, and that it denotes a 'genre of electronic music that became popular in the late 1990s'.

Kim Cascone's paper 'The Aesthetics of Failure' (Cascone, 2000) documented the emergence of glitch, created by self-taught composers who utilised the errors, or perhaps the 'dialect' (data drop-outs, bugs, clipping, quantization noise) of digital technology. Cascone warned academic institutions to keep abreast, not just of this musical 'movement' as he styled it, but of the self-taught composer trend.

In the same year, Rob Young surveyed the phenomenon of 'glitch music' and its locus ('underground digital music'), describing the genre as an 'urban environmental music… that reflects the depletion of 'natural' rhythms in the city experience, and in the striated plateau of the virtual domain' (Young, 2000).[1] Young considers the impulse that drives 'noise' music to be a social-revolutionary urge, a fulfilment of Jacques Attali's prophecies about music's contemporary task, which is the rejection of the nineteenth century cult of the god-composer, and the emphasis on 'purity' in the realisation of 'classic' works and the fidelity of recordings, by negating the undemocratic 'repetitive power' that capitalist societies manipulate through the cult of the concert and the recording (Attali, 1985).

In discussing the music of Merzbow (the composer Masani Akita), Paul Hegarty essays a 'theorization of noise', and cites Baudrillard's 'fractalisation of culture'[2], the proposition that all meanings are now haphazard, and radiate from no fixed point of reference (Hegarty, 2002). Hegarty suggests that 'noise music' can exist only at its first listening, after which it becomes familiar: becomes, indeed, 'music', instead of a threatening, chaotic Other, and thus, suggests Hegarty, noise music is that which 'tries not to definitively succeed' (Hegarty, 2002 p. 196). This aesthetic rejects Western Art music's goal of contributing to the world's store of beautiful things, (even though what is defined as 'beauty' is a changing quality).

Sherburne, in writing of the New York minimalist record label *12k*, discusses the genesis of microsound/glitch, calling it 'a strain of minimalist post-techno' (Sherburne, 2002, p. 171). Sherburne surveys some of microsound's pioneering practitioners, particularly Surge, whose music incorporates deliberate, human 'error', e.g. shifting a backbeat so that it 'sounds very wrong', as a 'creative catalyst' (Sherburne, 2002, p. 173).

---

[1] 'Striated plateau' is an image drawn from the work of Gilles Deleuze and Félix Guattari (Deleuze & Guattari, 1987) who use the model of the rhizome (rootless, node-less, proliferating) as a trope with which to analyse social phenomena and avoid traditional hierarchical or 'binary' conceptualisations, like the 'arboreal', meaning a tree with a dominating trunk and subordinate 'branches' of knowledge.
[2] *Fractalization* is another frequently-misused word in these critical texts; it is used to imply a sense of something 'fractured' or 'shattered', which it doesn't.

Janne Vanhanen observes how glitch has moved from being *avant-garde* to part of a recognised musical vocabulary (Vanhanen, 2003). Vanhanen, too, draws on the ideas of Gilles Deleuze to show that glitch is 'a concept in crisis': glitches *signify* an 'event' in music (an absence or an excess in the texture) without actually *being* an event. The issue facing the glitch artist, claims Vanhanen, is how to find a role as a creator controlling such an aleatoric, virtual structure.

Martijn Voorvelt's 'New Sounds, Old Technology' (Voorvelt, 2000) surveys 'pop experimentalism', and suggests that most innovators do not seek the latest electronic equipment and techniques, but rather concentrate on a thorough exploration of their existing means, including 'abuse' of instruments, equipment, and effects; he cites 'pop experimenter' Brian Eno's remark that the faults that develop in his equipment are 'rather interesting' (Voorvelt, 2000, p. 72). This is a pointer to the aleatoric component of glitch music, and its role in refreshing a composer's palette of materials with unexpected and perhaps unimaginable sonic pigments.[1]

Peter Manning (Manning, 2003) and Douglas Kahn (Kahn, 2003) provide historical perspectives to 'noise' inclusion in composition, and, while doing likewise, Phil Thomson also attempts to supply an academic glitch music aesthetic, arguing that microsound's granular materials themselves call for a new species of 'micro-analysis' (Thomson, 2004, p. 208).

Leonardo Music Journal devoted its 2003 issue to the topic 'Groove Pit and Wave'. In his Introduction, editor Nicolas Collins seemed to have the last word in the glitch debate, declaring that artefacts of recording – the stylus-traced grooves in vinyl records, the laser-plumbed pits in CDs, and the 'noise' these engender in the playback process - are now entrenched in contemporary music. 'Music isn't just *conveyed* through grooves, pits and waves. Music *is* grooves, pits and waves' (Collins, 2003, p. 3).

2.6 On the Topic of Recontextualizing Sound

In most contemporary discussions of glitch music, the works and ideas of Luigi Russolo, Pierre Schaeffer, and John Cage are likely to be highlighted. All were recontextualizers of noise, who shifted the borders between what is and what is not music, sometimes simply by renaming some sonic territory. Russolo's 1913 *Futurismo* manifesto advocated the

---

[1] Voorvelt calls this style 'pop *concrète*' (Voorvelt, 2000, p. 71).

assimilation of modern city-sounds as musical material '...the palpitation of valves, the coming and going of pistons, the howl of mechanical saws, the jolting of a tram on its rails...' (http://luigi.russolo.free.fr/arnoise.html). Russolo himself produced little music, inspired no compositional school or performance practice, yet is recognized, or at any rate claimed, as a proto-glitch composer. His appeal today may lie more in his bluster and his yen for iconoclasm.

Pierre Schaeffer's classic *Etude aux Chemins de Fer* sampled (as we now call it) the sounds of steam locomotives, and reorganized these into music-like ostinati, gestures, and phrases. By employing the rhetoric of music, Schaeffer caused these noises to *become* music. They were recontextualized from the urban *charivari* into the central discourse of music, under the aegis of *musique concrète*.

Arnold Schönberg styled John Cage 'an inventor of genius', rather than a composer.[1] Cage was certainly a polemicist, and his *4'33"* is a classic work of recontextualization, inviting the audience to attend only to the noises in and around the concert hall. Such sounds are thus incorporated into the music, like the noises produced by dust and scratches on the surface of a vinyl record.

The name of artist Marcel Duchamp appears in many texts on the subject of music that imports other 'objects'. Carol P. James writes of Duchamp's musical works; his ideal listener ('ear-eur') should be deaf, 'hearing' the music without physically listening to it, part of Duchamp's anti-Romantic philosophy of art, which aimed to free it from judgments based on taste (James, 1987). Duchamp's 'readymades', those ordinary objects re-contextualized by being displayed in an art gallery, provide a model for the inclusion of 'nasty noises' in musical contexts. Spin doctor Philip Jeck says that turntablism (see Chapter 3.8) created for him an opportunity 'to interact with the music without being a musician' (Dery, 1992, p. 63).

In 1989, John Oswald released his almost-legendary *Plunderphonics* CD, comprising 'revised performances' he had constructed from existing recordings of artists as diverse as Dolly Parton and Igor Stravinsky. Oswald was subsequently required to destroy the master tapes and all copies of this work, for breaching copyright laws. Oswald's 1985 paper presaged his ideas *re* the 'prerogative' of plundering pre-recorded sounds. 'After decades of

---

[1] This oft-quoted remark has a dubious provenance (Hicks, 1990, p. 134).

being the passive recipients of music… listeners now have the means to assemble their own choices…' (http://www.plunderphonics.com/xhtml/xplunder.html). A listener assembling an anthology on cassette tape from among a personal record collection, is 'composing' new music, Oswald asserts. A number of similar plunder-artists claim to have received no musical education beyond collecting, and presumably listening to, records (Shapiro, 2000; Sherburne, 2001). The originality of these works lies chiefly in disjunction, the apposition of unrelated, even conflicting texts. In the field of popular music, the primary plunder-genres are *hip-hip* and *techno* (see Chapter 3.6).

Chris Cutler's *Plunderphonia* argues that the received moral and legal values of art music 'impede and restrain… exciting possibilities in… the age of recording' (http://www.ccutler.com/writing/plunderphonia.shtml). Cutler's view is that the possibility of sound recording has rendered all inscribed sounds of any kind as material for composition, thus negating art music's requirement that new works must be completely original.

In several writings, Denis Smalley has evolved a lexicon for discussing the contextualization of sounds. Smalley's 'The Listening Imagination' (Smalley, 1992) and his 'Spectromorphology' (Smalley, 1997), both propose a set of terms for the analysis of electroacoustic music. Smalley's lexicon at present seems unwieldy, and not much adopted, but his comments on the aesthetic effect of sounds placed in contexts other than their origin, are significant.

On the topic of speculating about *why* there is a move to obliterate, distort and recontextualize the recorded past, Kevin Korsyn's applies Harold's Bloom's Freudian theory of 'the anxiety of influence' to the art of music, to show how composers 'clear imaginative space' for themselves by misreading their predecessors' influences: Brahms silences the tramp of the giant Beethoven by employing Beethoven's stylistic idioms, and shaping them to his own purposes (Korsyn, 1991). Paul Théberge, in *Any Sound You Can Imagine* (Théberge, 1997) proposes that the recontextualizing of sound results not in allusion to the past, but in emphasis on the current: making for 'multitemporality'. The ironization of old musics by citing them within new texts produces an 'endless awareness of the present' (Théberge, 1997, p. 206).

George Lipsitz, in *Dangerous Crossroads* (Lipsitz, 1994) writes of creativity that arises from 'mistaken readings' of musical cultures by those who engage with them, for example, pioneering (i.e. untrained) black jazz musicians who composed in 'difficult' key signatures, simply because the black keys of a piano were further apart and therefore easier to encompass; Lipsitz also notes the practice of hip-hip composers who deliberately make 'mistakes': '[A]s popular culture consumers, they have learned to take pleasure in the inconsistencies… that give recorded music its distinctive character' (Lipsitz, 1994, p. 167). Lipsitz does not examine the significance of the phrase 'take pleasure in', though amusement often arises from ironization. Nor does he examine the possibility that proto-jazz composers may have chosen less usual keys in order to locate their music away from the familiar tonal territory of the hymns, marches and ballroom dances that formed the popular music of their day.

Alexie Monroe compiles an 'icy' political agenda: that 'glitch' threatens corporate culture because of its coldly inhuman 'machine' aura (Monroe, 2003). Monroe suggests that 'sonists' (his word for laptop performer/composers) should make glitch music even 'sharper, icier… raw, jagged' to oppose the 'false warmth' of the 'authoritarian agendas' of corporate culture, which aim to tame and commodify all emerging musical genres (Monroe, 2003, p. p. 42). That glitch music ought to (if it does not explicitly) possess a Marxist reformative agenda is a question begged by most writers of the papers here mentioned.

2.7 On the Blurring of Boundaries between Art and Pop Musics

Record stores once had fewer bins. The divisions were 'Classical', 'Popular' and perhaps 'Spoken Word'. Today the categories have become almost countless; whole stores deal only in minor genres. We need to consider the blurry line that divides 'art' from 'popular' noise-based musics. The criterion may simply be the presence or absence of a steady pulse (Neill, 2002), but there is much socio-political baggage to examine as well. If a handful of writers on both sides of this cultural divide are to be heeded, it is not enough any more just to make, or even listen to, glitch music: a political stance is mandatory.

Mark Dery's *Rap* (Dery, 1988) explained a 'new' musical phenomenon to readers of *Keyboard* magazine, observing that 'Where John Zorn might rip off ideas from high-brow, low-brow and ethnic traditions, rap shoplifts the music *itself*… It's the ultimate in post-modern rag-picking' (Dery, 1988, p. 36). Rap's originality lay in juxtapositions, claimed Dery. Dery's use of pejorative terms like 'rip off', 'shoplift' and 'rag-picking' may be just the racy cant of pop-journalism, but Dery also begs the question of the necessity to perform this (sc)avenging, assuming on our behalf that it is a bold and even obligatory form of social redress by the marginalized.

Four years later, Dery explaining *turntablism* in *Keyboard*, remarked that its practitioners were 'at the intersection of *high* (read: white, Eurocentric, élitist) and *low* (read: non-white, non-Western, populist) traditions', but that these two 'nations' of music were contemporary forms of critical art, engaging with 'media cacophony' (Dery, 1992, p. 56). Dery's value-laden term 'cacophony' implies that these artists try to make sense of chaotic social 'noise'. It could be added that 'cacophony' denotes sonorities that seem harsh and discordant only to those who do not understand, or perhaps not wish to receive, messages so coded.

Joel Chadabe forecasts that soon, 'the antipodal positions of aristocratic and popular culture will no longer describe the music world', and asserts that computer music composers will use their skills to create 'situations' in which all people everywhere can 'participate meaningfully in a musical process'. Chadabe does not say why 'people everywhere' would *wish* to (Chadabe, 2000, p. 10). David Brackett's essay 'Where's It At?' (Bracket, 2002) attempts to show that the categories of 'high' and 'low' music have not collapsed or merged; they may exchange materials and absorb influences, but economics maintains their separation: pop remains a commodity, while art is sustained by the academy.

Tad Turner (Turner, 2003) argues that post-digital composers occupy a 'marginal genre'. By avoiding 'beat' in their music, they have been abandoned by the electronic dance community, yet have not sustained any dialogue with the academy, either. Tara Rodgers surveys the 'process and aesthetics' of sampling, and expresses her concerns about the 'politics of reconfiguration', but comes to no conclusions; her paper is chiefly a list of grumbles about aesthetic questions, which need to be addressed by 'further study' (Rodgers, 2003, p. 319).

2.8 Conclusion

In summary, these readings suggest that, with respect to the corpus of art music, 'glitch' remains a satellite genre, beaming on a wavelength to which the home planet is still not fully tuned.[1]

---

[1] Indeed, Phil Thomson declares that 'the new approaches to computer music production have yet to be taken seriously by research-based computer music institutions' (Thomson, 2004, 211).

CHAPTER 3: DEFINITIONS AND DERIVATIONS

3.0 Defining and Exampling Some Terms

Jargon is almost unavoidable when discussing technical or specialised matters, but we ought at least to ensure that the meaning of terms employed in this paper is clear to both writer and reader. Here are some definitions, and some discussion of the background to glitch music and its coevals. Sound examples referred to are inscribed on the enclosed CD, and listed in Appendix 1.

3.1 'Nasty' Noises

Ambrose Bierce called noise 'A stench in the ear'.[1] Noise is the pejorative term for any sound considered objectionable. A sound can be objectionable because it is physically unpleasant, even dangerous.[2] It can be unpleasant because it carries signifiers of alarm or distress - most people find a crying baby, or a keening dental drill, unpleasant.[3] Repetitive sounds can be objectionable - a dripping tap is the usual example - perhaps because they signify 'error', something demanding an immediate remedy. A repeatedly tapped pencil, or shoe, or a perpetually bleating automobile anti-theft alarm also can cause irritation, perhaps because such sounds demand attention, but to no purpose – a kind of 'error'. An AM radio receiver imprecisely tuned to the carrier wave of a transmitter station, a television receiving a weak signal, producing white noise and 'snow', are familiar modern irritant sounds.

A sound can be objectionable for aesthetic reasons. Elevator music, aircraft boarding music, mall music, restaurant and café music: bland musics, intended to soothe or comfort, can irritate by their very vapidity.[4] It is difficult to separate psychological factors from sheer aesthetic objections, however. Elevator music, for example, may be objectionable because elevators, and aircraft, take some people to destinations they dislike, among persons they would prefer to avoid, amid claustrophobic surroundings.

A listener may have social, as well as aesthetic objections, to the sounds of a political rally, a Deth Metal concert, a children's party, church-bells, a leaf-blower, mobile-phone alerts,

---

[1] In *The Devil's Dictionary* (Toronto: Coles, 1978 p. 90). His definition of *noise* continues, 'Undomesticated music. The chief product and authenticating sign of civilisation.'
[2] See 'The Acoustics of War' at http://www.cabinetmagazine.org/issues/5/acousticsofwar.php
[3] Locomotive horns are often tuned in dissonant 'clusters', or else assonant chords in unusual keys like D#. See http://atsf.railfan.net/airhorns/k5la.html
[4] Classical (*sic*) music was used, with some success, to discourage gangs from loitering in the shopping malls and subways of Montreal, Toronto, Edmonton and Moncton. See *National Post* (Canada) December 14, 1998.

certain mispronunciations, or belching. These sounds are 'nasty' because they occur out of context: in this case, what is and is not welcome into the personal space of a certain hearer.

'Nasty' noises, then, are sounds in the wrong place. Or in the wrong music.

3.2 Glitch Music

Glitch music is conventional electroacoustic music whose sound-source is confined to a single aural domain: the sounds of error and failure. Glitch is a 'sound-world'. It is not a technique or style of composition. Whether a glitch musical text is machine-generated by algorithms of chance, or assembled piecemeal by a human artist, the result will be the same: a work whose sonorities denote electronic error and breakdown. Glitch is electrical-engineering jargon for 'error', especially a transient event, like a brief but significant increase in line voltage. The 'nasty noises' incorporated in glitch music carry signification of such malfunction, and of failure. Glitches are sourced from audio devices, e.g. a purposely defaced, skipping, or fast-forwarded, CD the back-tracking lead-in groove of a vinyl record and many difficult-to-identify electronic hiccups.

Glitch can also derive from any sampled sound, sliced up into fragments, filtered with software like *Buzz*, and redistributed as gesture or percussive accent. Thus, glitch is a style of *recontextualization* of musical material.

Digitally-derived sounds may signify 'error' to only a small proportion of listeners, those who have spent years working with digital equipment, audio and otherwise, and who recognise echoes of device breakdown.[1] Nonetheless, the disruptive placement of a gesture, whether it is a true 'glitch', or the stacked, truncated and gated samples of seven synthesized kick-drum beats, brings 'error' into the structure of the piece itself, another glitch technique.

The superficial difference between popular and art-music glitch is the presence or absence of persistent pulse (Byrne, 2002, p. 10; Sherburne, 2002, p. 172; Neill, 2002, p. 5; Thomson, 2004, p. 212). Compare the styles of SND, and Alva Noto. The 'dance-ability' of some glitch might be questionable: it seems to have inherited from disco/techno only its rhythmic conventions. It is interesting to observe how even the most 'abstract' (another sub-genre of electronica) of glitch composers usually repeats ('loops') a glitch phrase or

---

[1] '[In] 1996… he accidentally dropped his … Walldorf 4-Pole filter, which, in its newly damaged state, began to generate seductively unpredictable crackles…' (*The Wire*, 196: June, 2000)

gesture, recalling Peter Kivy's assertion that music is but 'the fine art of repetition' (Kivy, 1993, p. 328). Otherwise, unfamiliar material might seem like a mistake. Glitch, microsound, techno: the topology of these musics is the loop. They chant in motoring, machine-inflected languages. Their pulse is not systolic, derived from heart-beats, but cyclic, like the media whereon they reside: discs, cylinders, tape arcing from spool to spool. As eternal as a prayer wheel, as subtle as the music of the spheres.

It is also interesting to note that by 2003, in his 'Introduction: Groove, Pit and Wave', Nicolas Collins, Editor in Chief of *Leonardo Music Journal* saw need to distance his discourse from networks of 'low' musics by crucifying the word *glitch* high inside scare quotes, and naming it a 'pop' style (Collins, 2003, p. 2). *Microsound* has more academic resonance, it seems.

3.3 Microsound

Another term used for glitch music is *microsound*, but there is a subtle difference: *microsound* tends to be a product of the university-based and research-oriented composer, prominent among these being Curtis Roads (Roads, 2001) and Kim Cascone (Cascone, 2000). Microsound is extensively discussed in Phil Thomson's paper 'Atoms and Errors' (Thomson, 2004); the style is characterised by the use of extremely brief time scales, typically a tenth of a second or less, and by *granulation*, digital slicing of sound into tiny sub-sections, akin to medical *microtomy*, the slicing of tissue into tiny segments for microscopic examination. The *.microsound* discussion list at http://www.microsound.org/ has links to sound files of experimental projects, for example, bufferFuct. With reference to this project, Kim Cascone's abstract reads:

> 'I recently spent a month at STEIM[1] developing a sound library called 'bufferFuct'. The idea was to take bugs found in LiSa, their live sampling software, and use them in the creation of new sounds. Most of the samples I developed are beat-oriented but this doesn't mean that the final pieces have to use beats. All styles of microsound are welcome.' (http://www.microsound.org/bufferfuct/)

Entry instructions were:

> 'Using only the material found on the hotline server (in the 'bufferFuct_ProjectFolder' dir) create a new work no longer than 6 minutes in length. As usual, feel free to mutate, mangle, destroy, induce failure in, and generally further fuck up the samples to your hearts (*sic*) content.' (http://www.microsound.org/bufferfuct/)

---

[1] *STudio for Electro-Instrumental Music*: http://www.steim.org/steim/info.html

3.4 Noise Music

Glitches are by definition accidental (few engineers *want* glitches in their circuits), and brief. *Noise Music* as such is constructed from longer, often sustained, electronic (and other) 'nastiness'. Best-known exponent is Japanese sound-artist Merzbow. The borders between this genre and glitch are blurred, though the word 'unpleasant' often occurs in descriptions of Noise Music. Noise here is *literally* nasty noise, sounds that many listeners would call objectionable, if only because of their merciless volume level, though others might enjoy them precisely *because* they are traditionally 'marginalised', shunned sounds. In contrast, glitch music may seem somehow gentler, even despairing.

3.5 lowercase music

> 'Lowercase recordings are often based on scientific subjects: an amplified anthill, a mobile phone running out of power and the soft pops of bacteria being flash-frozen in dry ice and methanol… The sounds are then chopped up, looped, stretched, repeated or delayed to create minimalist, near-silent musical compositions. The results demand deep, concentrated listening, but can be surprisingly affecting.' (Kahney, 2002).

This style seems descended from some hi-fi buffs' hobby of the 1950s, recording 'tiny' sounds on open-reel tape, with shotgun microphones, and then amplifying these enormously. Such sounds were not, however, consciously fashioned into musical works.[1] For example, 'Nimb #20' by Toshimaru Nakamura, is constructed from sounds produced by an audio mixer feeding back into itself, with no external input material.

3.6 Techno

In the lexicon of contemporary electronic music, every genre and sub-genre seems connected to every other, so that it is impossible to draw up a 'family tree' showing the *ur-genre* from which all others descend. A Deleuze-style rhizomic network might be a better and more politically correct model of connectedness. Techno, as such, sprouts from post-disco dance music. A studio-crafted, chiefly instrumental, synthesizer-based style, Techno was aimed at disco disc-jockeys (DJs) who played very long sets, but who had adventurous musical tastes. There are many sub-styles, e.g. Detroit *techno*; UK *acid-techno*, but the experimental wing of techno, perhaps of more interest to art-music composers, is called Intelligent Dance Music (IDM), as well as *intelligent techno, listening techno, art techno, experimental techno*, or *braindance*.[2]

---

[1] J.G. Ballard's 1958 short story *Track 12* concerns a 'microsound experimenter' who poisons his wife's lover, and makes him listen to the amplified sound of their kissing (!) while he dies. In *Penguin Science Fiction* ed. Brian Aldiss (Penguin, 1965).
[2] IDM's dance-focussed detractors call it 'dolphin music'.

Another catch-all term for experimental-style techno is *electronica*. Glitch music discographies frequently cite the pioneering works of Alva Noto (Carsten Nicolai) and Oval (Marcus Popp), who compose in these styles. Electronica practitioners blend into bands, collaborate on albums, perform, and disperse, with the regularity of clouds. Band names are suitably High Modernist-Minimalist and technology-derived (Autechre, Aphex Twin), and many are one-musician operations (Plex, Modex, Pole). Retail availability of affordable electronic musical instruments and recording equipment has allegedly 'democratised' music-making;[1] hence, the vast number of practitioners, and the inseparable link of electronic art music to popular music: for example, the band Kraftwerk. Dance-music makers have provided a huge pool of self-appointed Beta-testers for laboratory–derived techniques, like *sampling*.

3.7 Sampling

Strictly speaking, *sampling* is simply the recording of audio material. As it is used in the context of electronic music, however, sampling denotes a procedure of careful selection, excision, modification, and employment of a sonic event, akin to clipping an image from a magazine page, perhaps colouring or otherwise modifying it, copying it many times, and constructing a collage, tessellation, or other artwork from that single 'sample'.

A legacy of World War II was the open-reel sound recorder, which used iron-powder coated plastic tape as a storage medium, a material that could be simply, if laboriously, edited with scissors and Sellotape. Pierre Schaeffer, after experiments with editing pre-vinyl discs, saw the compositional possibilities of such a medium. In 1948, Schaeffer 'sampled' locomotive sounds, and constructed from these a sonic collage, and a genre: *musique concrète*. Schaeffer's choice of locomotives as sonic material is interesting; a 'pulse', a range of *obbligati*, even a noise-derived 'Alberti bass', are available, and he exploits them. Already, with Schaeffer and his Batignolles experiment, electronic music 'chugs'; repetition is part of the culture. Some of Schaeffer's later work became more object-oriented and stochastic, the samples briefer, recontextualized, and stereophonic. Schaeffer's colleague (until 1958) Pierre Henry pursued a less 'test-tube' style of composition: many of his electronic works import extra-musical ideas from literature, or from Dada styles of art. For example, Henry's *Variations pour une porte et un soupir* (*Variations for a door and a sigh*, 1963), which in 1974 became a ballet.

---

[1] See for example Braut, Christian *The Musician's Guide to MIDI*. Almeda: SYBEX, 1994, p. xxxiv, and Huber, D.M. *Modern Recording Techniques*. Burlington: Elziver, 2005, p. 8.

The arrival of microchip, and hence, digital technology, brought the *sampler*, former electronic laboratory equipment, now packaged and consumerised, with integrated keyboard.[1] By the 1980s, samplers were within the financial reach of most Western musicians (Goodwin, 1988, p. 37). The 'drum machine' was especially popular: endless, complex beats were available without the fatigue of beating a surface. Most samplers offered 'licks' (brief melodic figures) of guitar, brass, or voice. Others, e.g. the Yamaha SY series, used samples of true orchestral instruments, striving towards a 'natural' sound. Due to the limitations of the digital technology of the time (early samplers were 8-bit devices, with a maximum one second's worth of sample time, at 33 kHz), the typical sample was brief, and its sound artificial. Yet it could be replicated and distributed across a keyboard, providing a performable set of pitches with adventurous timbres. Brevity may also have helped to disguise the source of the material, and evade copyright issues. The keyboard-execution heritage of sampling also accounts for the essentially percussive, non-legato character of much electronic music.

A generation of musicians who grew up listening to electronically fabricated timbres that were trying to sound natural might well be ripe for artistic apostasy: choosing to sanctify sounds that seem as *unnatural* as possible. They might indeed be ready to 'worship' glitch (Young, 2000).

3.8 Turntablism

Turntablism denotes the performance practice of improvising dance music, using short excerpts from vinyl recordings. The Technics SL1200 record player is the favoured instrument. It can be set in 'neutral', spun freely with the fingers, then started instantly, a procedure required for pre-broadcast track-cueing. This feature was exploited by hiphop disco-jockeys, who were able to rapidly locate and cue tiny sections of individual tracks ('scratching'), then play just these 'cuts' (excerpts). By using two turntables and a mixer, rapidly cross-fading from one recording to the other, DJs could continually devise new 'grooves' (ostinato-like figures), ideal for non-stop disco-type dancing.

Turntablism spawned an entire school of studio-based music, loosely called *plunderphonics*, the (controversial) fabrication of 'new' music from samples excerpted from existing recordings (Oswald, 1985; Cutler, 1994). This style is sometimes called *bricolage*, from a

---

[1] Australia's Fairlight CMI was the world's first digital sampler, and was bought by Stevie Wonder, among others, in 1979.

parallel arts practice which constructs sculptures from materials 'at hand', as distinct from those sought for, or even 'found', e.g. collage. A whole generation has grown up with their Baby Boomer parents' considerable collection of vinyl records 'at hand'.

Much *plunderphonia* seems driven by nostalgia. Steve Roden, when writing about his piece *OTR* that was constructed from his mother's collection of 1960s-era, 45 r.p.m. vinyl records, remarked:

> 'I like the idea that this quiet, repetitive music is a kind of aesthetic mirror for all those nights my mother fell asleep listening to these records, the dark room humming with the minimalist rhythmic sound of a needle stuck in the last groove, endlessly circling the record label until morning' (Roden, 2003, p. 86).

Roden is one of many glitch artists interested in foregrounding the surface noise of vinyl records to create new works:

> 'The aging processes of a human and a piece of well-played vinyl are not so different—one is covered with wrinkles and scars, the other with scratches and fingerprints. These images begin to redefine the surface as a new surface or new persona, a new face built upon the old one, a new song composed of disturbances and interruptions' (Roden, 2003, p. 86).

Thus, surface noise and scratches, *as* scratches, are not nasty noises if they are recontextualized as members of the set of events that comprise the musical text.

Since 2000/2001, a sub-genre of turntablism has emerged: mash-up. The object of this plunder-genre is to juxtapose the most unlikely styles of music by taking the vocal from one record and the 'bed', or instrumental backing from another: Madonna sings with Kraftwerk, Johnny Cash backs Rapper Nas, Bennie Goodman plays with the Beastie Boys, Jimi Hendrix performs with Rapper Tupac; the style is often hip-hop/rap (http://www.mashupradio.com).

3.9 Recontextualization

Finally, we arrive at this cumbersome word that nonetheless could serve as a banner under which much postmodern art could march. Recontextualization signifies the taking of an object from its original setting and placing it in another, with the intention of creating new meanings for both the object and its new surrounds. The new meaning is often ironic, wryly amusing, playful, rather than uplifting or revelatory: the antithesis of the critical rules of Modernism. Take a handful of seashells, and a photograph of Elvis Presley. Gum the shells around the portrait's perimeter. *Gastropodia* + Presley = *kitsch*.

This is a Hegelian equation of creativity: thesis + antithesis = synthesis.[1] It is also the Duchampian 'junk is art if you view it as art' credo. But junk can be simultaneously art *and* refuse. Its membership of the set of the discarded, the unwanted, the extruded, intersects with its membership of the selected, and the published, when located within an art-work. It also possesses that enigmatic quality residing in every recontextualized object that allows the 'reader' of any artistic text to experience and decipher its meaning personally. Barthes's 'death-of-the-author' assertion allows no ultimate meaning for any text, beyond one's perception of it, at this time, and in this place.

> 'We know now that a text is not a line of words releasing a single 'theological' meaning (the 'message' of the Author-God) but a multi-dimensional space in which a variety of writings, none of them original, blend and clash. The text is a tissue of quotations drawn from the innumerable centres of culture' (Barthes, 1977, p. 171).

(In which case, Barthes' pronouncements are only *one* of the meanings of his text. So what does he mean? How can one cite him?)

The recontextualization of CD jitter within the narrative of a musical work draws on both the signifier of error that arrives with the jitter, and its re-valuation as an art-object within its new setting of an art-music narrative. The jitter is rhythmical, motoring, and as such, a recognisable musical elemental, a quotation drawn from the 'innumerable centres of culture'. Its welcome into the text of the music negates its signification of 'error'; no longer glitch, perhaps *gemütglitch*. By recontextualizing a feral sound and taming it, glitch seems to be sliding downwards, from sub-genre, to style, to mannerism, to ornament. Mr John Cage, has, of course, the Last Word on all such matters: 'The History of Art is simply a history of getting rid of the ugly, by entering into it, and using it.' (Cage, cited in Kostelanetz, 1987, p. 211).

---

[1] Hegelian: refers to the ideas of Georg Wilhelm Friedrich Hegel (1770-1831), German philosopher, who is credited with this three-step 'dialectic' used to analyse evolution in human cultures; in fact it owes more to the ideas of his followers, like Marx and Engels, and Hegel himself is alleged to have borrowed his dialectic from Fichte (1762-1814).

CHAPTER 4: GLITCH AND GLITCHING

4.0 Why Is Glitch Music?

Why has glitch music happened? My suggestions for the advent of glitch music follow here.

4.1 The Never Ending Story

That glitch music is part of music's never-ending search for new means and materials of expression. In orchestral compositional terms, it is an 'extended technique', akin to writing parts at the extreme range of instruments, or calling for them to be used in an unconventional manner: flutter-tongue with tuba, *glissando* with clarinet, bowing the strings behind the bridge of a cello. For glitch music, instead of striking a note on an electronic keyboard, one might use the sound created by the keyboard's circuitry when it is switched on: the *click*, *thud*, or *crack* heard in the speakers when an electric current jumps across the contacts of the power switch; and this sound can also be digitally dismembered.

4.2 Do It Yourself

That glitch music is a reaction against the de-personalizing effect of ready-made sounds and processes, e.g. software like *SoundHack*, or *Cloud Generator*, which modify audio files, resulting in timbres or effects that have become clichéd; or synthesizer modules that offer thousands of readymade 'patches'.

4.3 Error = Individuality

That it has become too easy to achieve conventional perfection. Music-making has been packaged; one can now readily produce the effects that others once strove for.

> 'Now [glitch] is all just another set of sounds for synthesizers and software manufacturers… I don't really care for what it's become or the ease which people have figured out how to make [glitch]…' Kid-606 (Shapiro, 2000, p. 12).

Glitch uses software suites like *Buzz* (http://buzzmachines.com) and *Audiomulch* (http://www.audiomulch.com). At least one glitch sound library is available: M-Audio offers *Sounds Logikal*, samples for 'exploiting technological failures and glitches in the pursuit of new dance music' (http://www.m-audio.com/products/en_us/Vol14SoundLogickal-main.html). A glitch how-to is available at http://remixmag.com/tech_features/remix_fractal_tendencies). It has become increasingly difficult for even a glitch artist to achieve distinction from the mob. Only in error, in deviance, was there, for a time, any personal 'signature' available to an electronic composer, but this has already been packaged.

Or rather, only in *reference* to deviance. Glitch music is carefully put together, and published for consumption. Its materials are merely *signifiers* of error. The ultimate, purist glitch musical work would be absent, because the means of its inscription and publication would have failed.

4.4 Refracted Meanings

That glitch, and turntablism, while containing an element of 'recognition' that acknowledges the authority of previous musics (and sonic apparatus) by quoting from them, chiefly seek to ironise, to refract past meanings through a present lens, derive new visions, and so dissolve, or diminish, previous authority. This impulse is iconoclastic, with the same revisioning intent as the anti-art of Dada, redefining the object and its context so that they are understood afresh, but distancing also the authority of art, and the artist.

The iconoclastic 'Art of Noises' *manifesto* of 1913, by Futurist Luigi Russolo uses a highly emotive language, as though all past, as well as all existing art, is personally offensive to the writer:

> 'Away! Let us break out since we cannot much longer restrain our desire to create finally a new musical reality, with a generous distribution of resonant slaps in the face, discarding violins, pianos, double-basses and plaintive organs. Let us break out!' (http://luigi.russolo.free.fr/arnoise.html).

Futurismo's worship of technology was less to do with admiring machinery itself, than a violent and adolescent repulsion of authority, an essentially Romantic gesture of renunciation by embracing an antithesis. Russolo's *intonarumori* were not after all automatic devices, but instruments of musical expression, meant to be played by human hands. *The Art of Noises* manifesto has a touch of simple contrariness about it. Russolo's manifesto is interesting as an historical document, but his program of musical reform is unlikely ever to be implemented in exactly the manner he demands.

Russolo was a painter, not a composer: not a few glitch-makers are visual artists, with a painter's or sculptor's urge to engage with and refashion physical materials, to impose their own vision on clay, stone, vinyl. One such is Christian Marclay, a turntablist who 'manipulates information to generate new meanings… meta-music, music about music…'

(Dery, 1992, p. 57). Marclay is uncomfortable with the label 'musician', and Dery calls him a 'deconstructionist'.

4.5 On Deconstruction

Deconstruction is a technique of literary criticism that questions the authority of a text by revealing its multiple and conflicting meanings. The word is increasingly used as a synonym for 'dismantle', or 'dissect', in the sense of stripping down an entity into its essential components: aesthetic hot-rodding. Marclay is a defacer of vinyl records, and his 'deconstructionist' approach is a 'mediation on sound made saleable in a market economy, vinyl as fetish, appropriation as creative act… and the reanimation of the recorded dead as techno-voodoo.' Allowing for journalistic hyperbole, Marclay, among the other spin doctors described in this 1992 article, is still cast as a revolutionary, the 'out there' stylus-brother of the hip-hop rapper, both of them standing at a crossroads, at 'the intersection of (high) *élitist* and (low) populist traditions'. Glitching (defacing, disrupting, ploughing up the smooth plateaux of past musical texts) is here a political act, even a religious one, not only necessary, but inevitable. Recording has meant the death of music, suggests Marclay, all music has now been written, no more instrumentalists will be required.[1] The glitcher must keep music alive by recontextualization, like the curator of a museum endlessly rearranging a finite number of specimens in a multiplicity of 'themed' exhibitions.

4.6 The Decay of Composition

Marclay also claims that, due to digital sampling technology, 'musicians are a vanishing species… the phenomenon of the DJ may be a last desperate way of saying… we're not totally irrelevant.' Digital sampling technology, predicts Marclay, means that in the future, consumers will buy music only as raw material and refashion it, using their home sampler, to their own taste. 'The whole idea of owning cultural artifacts (*sic*) will be defeated' (Dery, 1992, p. 59). Joel Chadabe, too, writes of a 'crossroads', or perhaps a confluence, where 'high' and 'low' electronic musics are now blending. Chadabe demands that future electronic composers 'use their elite knowledge and skill to create situations in which members of the public without that knowledge and skill can participate meaningfully in a musical process… interactive composition… a new approach to high art' (Chadabe, 2000, p. 10).

---

[1] cf. Fredric Jameson: '[W]riters and artists of the present day will no longer be able to invent new styles and worlds – they've already been invented…' (Jameson, 1983, p. 117).

4.7 Blitz

Kim Cascone, in his much-cited essay 'The Aesthetics of Failure' warned that 'in order to help better understand current trends in electronic music, the researchers in academic centres must keep abreast of these trends' (Cascone, 2000, p. 18). But who has suggested that 'academic' electronica composers are not 'abreast'? In 2000, the Digital Musics Jury of Cyberarts 2000 issued the following statement:

> 'It's audible that our critics in the academic electroacoustic community have a visceral dislike of popular culture… the entire value of the now defunct Computer Music Prize stemmed from its historical role as a refuge from, a direct opponent of, and a zone of aesthetic superiority over the inescapable vulgarity of popular music… Academic composers, bless them, insist on maintaining a distance from the extreme complexities of modern digital music… This can only be because their extreme minority isolation is experienced not as a fatal disability but as a valued attribute' (Eshun, 2000, p. 194-195).

There's a bit more of this rather patronising discourse, and then Eshun declares '[C]ommercialism doesn't corrupt music as academics believe… it multiplies and mutates all media into networks of audiosocial desire' (the Deleuzian rhizome again). Eshun concludes by lauding a winning microsound entry (Carsten Nicolai's *20' to 2000*) which 'embraces a tendency towards… audio austerity'. (Eshun is another who uses 'deconstruct' to mean 'strip away', 'expose' or 'reveal'.) Nicolai's entry, writes Eshun, 'typifies the tendency towards collaboration that's… post-media practice'. Eshun cites media theorist Howard Slater, whose term 'post-media operator' describes any composer who chooses to 'operate' outside the monetary and conceptual constraints of the institutional control of the music industry and the media, 'thereby eluding the dominant repressive models of inherited subjectivity', which seems as near as never-mind to a description of an academic composer (Eshun, 2000, p. 200-201). The word 'historical' in Eshun's text seems as carefully chosen, and as chilling, as the word 'operator' in lieu of 'artist'. Glitch, then, may not only be the sound of a music-making device failing: it may be the death-rattle of electronic composition itself. Music-making retreats from joy to adopt a stern agenda of reform: from the sublime to the medicinal.

4.8 Glitz

Despite such sniping at the academy, every pop journalist writing about electronica seems anxious to demonstrate intellectual street-cred by high-brow name-dropping (Derrida is *passé*, Deleuze is *chic*; Baudrillard, Attali and Adorno always march in the parade), by adopting a trendy jargon of 'auralities', 'performatives', and 'plateaux', and by adding a tough-bunny dollop of carefully PC obscenity. Sound-artists of the genre, too, hitch up to the tow-bar of any cultural Thunderbird:

> 'The real name of the piece [*Baudelaire*] is *Baudrillard* (French post-modern theorist). The Whitney printed it wrong and in the spirit of things we just went with it :) .' Matthew Allen, a.k.a. Plex. (Personal communication, 27 July, 2004. Includes emoticon.)

A sublime implementation of the glitch aesthetic: even the *title* is an error.

4.9 Sitz

Is glitch dying? The 2004 Prix Ars Digital Musics jury cautiously observed, 'No art form can leap forward every year. 2004 was characterized by the sensations of a holding pattern: you circle above the airport […] yet, even in this uncomfortable position of going nowhere, enjoying the opportunity to study the ground below in detail. To be blunt, nothing sounded very new or surprising…' (Toop *et al*, 2004, p. 073).

New and surprising are High Modernist standards of artistic worth, and the mere consolidation or assimilation of a genre cannot today be of interest, surely? The word 'glitch' appears nowhere in the judges' nine-page commentary, yet of the fifteen sound examples on the CD accompanying the Prix Ars compendium, twelve are glitch or microsound works, or at any rate, draw on glitch, noise, or recontextualization techniques.

Nor does the word 'glitch' occur in any of the successful entrants' commentaries on their work. Anne Laplantine's *Anne: Hamburg* consists of her banal electric-guitar strummings digitally cut up and reassembled 'blind', including editing clicks at the junctions of samples. Laplantine describes her compositional approach as 'the confrontation between the accidents created by this random process and my possible control over them… like contemporary writing, including incidents and errors' (Leopoldseder *et al*, 2004, p. 089). Glitch would appear to have established itself at least as a mannerism, if not a discrete style, if the *Prix Ars* musics represent the cutting-edge of digital audio composition.

4.10 Intertextuality, and the Anxiety of Influence

The 2004 Prix Ars judges continued the academy-bashing, observing that 'consequential music can be produced by people who do not consider themselves full-time artists, who may be producing crafted sounds simply because they have acquired a laptop with access to a variety of music software… a kind of new-technological-folk music that is no longer the sole domain of the schooled musician' (Leopolseder *et al*, 2004, p. 073).

And compare:

> 'I believe that there could be Beethovens and Mozarts in the ghettoes… who never surface because they can't get access to the tools of music…' Tom Silverman, hop-hip record producer and publisher (Dery, 1988, p. 56).

Now, it is not impossible that some or many of these once-marginalised crafters of sounds may nurse a covert or even a blatant agenda of revenge or reclamation against the musical establishment. Their 'consequential music' may be intended to challenge the dominance of 'schooled' musicians of previous musics, especially pop-music artists of the stature of The Beatles, whose practical accomplishment equates with superior formal music study. Emerging artists might seek to redress a perceived aesthetic powerlessness. A generation of sound organisers feeling defeated or at least disadvantaged by the weight of the past might invent an entire genre whose intent is to destabilise the power-base of all recorded material. 'It's like the whole history of recorded sound is waiting there for us to murder' Rapper Matt Black (Dery, 1988, p. 37). There may even be a Freudian element of rebellion; artists symbolically defying the authority of their Baby-Boomer parents, Generation X, that claims to have invented and permanently defined pop-music, leaving nothing for any subsequent 'low' music-maker to contribute.

Slicing up, distorting, misrepresenting the works of forbears is also a bid to carve out some personal territory. Turntablist Otomo Yoshihide 'savagely (de)constructs jazz' (Shapiro 1999, p. 40). Art music sound organisers, too, strive for such *lebensraum*. Ekkehard Ehlers, described as an 'electronics perpetrator', released in 2000 his album *Betrieb*, which dealt with 'movements between closed systems' (that is, autonomous musical compositions) by breaking down works (that is, *recordings* of works) by Schoenberg and Charles Ives. 'Every track is created out of one source and the loops are layered in a dodecaphonic-like structure' says Ehlers, a teacher of 'time based media' at Stuttgart's Merz Academy for Design, whose musical education was 'record collecting' (Sherburne, 2000, p. 12). In the words of Kevin Korsyn, such artists, 'by misreading one another… clear imaginative space for themselves' (Korsyn, 1991, p. 6).

Korsyun's 1991 paper, 'Towards a New Poetics of Musical Influence' took Harold Bloom's Freud-influenced theory of the 'anxiety of influence' among poets, and applied it to composers (Bloom, 1973). Deconstructive readings of musical texts had alarmed some musicologists; the new theory of *intertextuality* suggested that no musical work could ever be analysed as a discrete entity. Each work was the product of influence, of uncounted and perhaps uncountable other texts, a 'rendezvous of texts'. Korsyn's paper suggested a model for musical analysis, drawing on Bloom's theory of influence. '[P]oetry becomes a psychic battlefield, an Oedipal struggle against one's poetic fathers, in which poets seek to repress and exclude other poems' (Korsyn, 1991, p. 8). To do this, suggested Bloom, poets misread each other, that is, rather than directly quoting, or even alluding to previous works, they transmute influence into a personal idiom. 'Strong' poets are those who create genuinely original works, and achieve their voice this way. Others achieve weaker works, and their voice is less clear. Bloom identifies six modes (Bloom calls them 'reversionary ratios') of achieving misreadings, among them *tessera*, literally, a mosaic tile or cube. The influence of an earlier artist is to be found, fragmented and dispersed, in the text of a later. Musicologists can then identify these fragments and reassemble them, like a mosaic, to identify the elements of influence of the 'senior' artist.

Korsyn demonstrates the musical application of *tessera* at some length, by analysing Brahms's bid, in his *Romanze* op. 118 no. 5 to shrug off the influence of Chopin's *Berceuse*, op. 57. The 'fragments' that characterise the *Berceuse,* its ostinato, its truncated theme of only four bars ending in 'mid-air', its recurring five-note *motif*, are taken by Brahms and used to create a more extended discourse, as though Chopin had not said enough with the ideas he chose. This is, however, more than simple granulation and recontextualization; what makes the Brahms *Romanze* 'canonical' i.e. discrete, autonomous, unique, in one word, *original*, is that Brahms also ironizes Chopin's harmonic structure, framing the *Berceuse* fragments so that they become an episode *within* the larger harmonic scheme of the *Romanze*. Brahms creates a new image with old materials; the tiles retain Chopin's pigments, but they glow within a new conceptualisation by the 'junior' artist. To leap a century or so forward and across several musical cultures, we hear an echo of Hegel again:

> 'I'm with everybody who steals stuff, because in my book, one plus one equals three... when you take one sound and add it to a second sound, you create a third sound' Steve Ett, hip-hop producer (Dery, 1988, p. 48).

4.11 Glitchers on Glitching

4.12 My Glitch

My interest in glitch music, as such, began when I was composing my first electroacoustic work during my postgraduate studies at the Sydney Conservatorium of Music in 2003. I had listened to a great many electronic and electroacoustic works (mostly 'anthology' CDs) to try to catch up with what had been happening in the three decades since 1972, when I created my first experimental work, using an open-reel tape-recorder, a number of clocks, my voice, a cymbal, and a snare drum.

The piece I now produced, thirty-one years after, was *Stingle*. I knew that some sort of 'new sound' would be expected of me, as a composer in this medium, and for *Stingle* I used a technique that I believed I had discovered, which was 'skipping' (or *sautage*, as I playfully called it), fast-forwarding through the tracks of an audio CD (a CD of my own compositions, let it be added), recording the resulting aleatory material, and using these as compositional elements.

My next piece, *Baleani*, deconstructed the text of a cheap electronic organ, built in 1976, by setting its native 'nasty' sounds against itself, as well as sounds produced when its circuits and components (modified by myself) were pushed outside their comfort zones to produce distortion and other 'unwanted' sounds: erroneous sonorities ironising the instrument's lower-middle-brow musical culture. I thought that this idea, too, was original. The concept followed on from my installation, 'Art Music for the Young Audience – Why Not?', on display in the foyer of the Faculty of Creative Arts at the University of Wollongong for some days in 1999. For this work, I dismantled a number of children's musical toys, sampling the tinny sounds they produced and composing these into a twenty minute electroacoustic work, the varying audio output of which then triggered these instruments and other devices.[1] I thought that this, too, was an original idea.

In 2003, I composed several works for my album *Tunnel Music*, among them *Not in North Sydney*, an extemporised *opera buffo* duet. I added gestures to this later, created by smashing glass jars and bottles. This is perhaps noise music or even *musique concrète*, but I had not yet heard of glitch.

When I presented *Baleani* at a Conservatorium composers' seminar, the discussion afterwards included the remark that my work sounded like *glitch music*. Embarrassed now, that my ideas were so unoriginal, I thought I'd better find out what glitch music was. I read of the CD-skipping work of Yasunao Tone, the 'circuit-bending' of Reed Ghazala, the microsonics of Kim Cascone, the 'Clicks 'n' Cuts' of Oval, SND, Noto, and the whole glitch 'movement'. What I wanted to know next was, *why* is glitch?

---

[1] Nasty noises created by this installation annoyed many Faculty of Creative Arts staff. My installation often had its power-plug pulled out by lecturers from nearby classrooms.

What do other glitchers say about glitching?

4.13 *Spirit Trace*

Robin Rimbaud, a.k.a. Scanner, wrote of his work 'Spirit Trace':

> Spirit Trace… is a musical homage to the pioneering researchers of Electronic Voice Phenomena… [This] refers to the sounds and voices that can be heard in ambient audio recordings, arguably those of the deceased… I focused on the anomalies found on blank digital recording media of very personal locations in London. What one hears is the highly amplified sound of the ghosts in the machine, the spaces in between the zeros and ones, corrupted, distorted, processed and reconstructed into this work - literally, the sound of digital 'silence' ' (Rimbaud, 2003, p. 86).[1]

4.14 *Study 1.0 (FM)*

As for 'the sound of digital silence', Matthew Burtner's *Study 1.0 (FM)* is part of a composition project that 'questions the nature of the radio medium in general and particularly the role it plays in forming the content of a musical signal' (Burtner, 2003, p. 34). Burtner used a small frequency-modulated transmitter to send an unmodulated (nil data) carrier-wave over a short distance. This signal passed through a receiver, and was then fed back into the transmitter, to be sent again, an endless loop of non-content. The result, wrote Burnter, is that 'the listener hears the compounding of the inherent noise generated in the process of transference. The growth of the systemic noise moves from the periphery of the music, a by-product of the media, to the central focus of the musical material. We hear the resonance of the FM band grow from noise, the intoning of the medium' (Burtner, 2003, p. 40).

In radio broadcasting jargon, silence is 'dead air': the absence of any signal modulating the carrier wave, usually through equipment malfunction. In broadcasting culture, silence therefore, is a glitch. Silence should exist only as an event between closely adjacent audible sonic events, a brief, punctuating device. If nothing is happening, then audiences stop listening and tune their receiver elsewhere, a Very Bad Thing in commercial broadcasting especially.

Frequency-modulated broadcasts are theoretically noise-free, or rather, interference-free. The signal must be of sufficient strength to be 'fully quieting', that is, to over-ride the chaotic radiations of the universe that would otherwise be heard as white noise. (This capacity of an FM receiver to 'listen' to only the strongest of a number of detected signals

---

[1] This work can be heard on the CD accompanying *Leonardo Music Journal* Issue 13, 2003.

on the same frequency is known as the 'capture effect'). The amplitude of the FM carrier wave is constant, and not subject to fluctuation by added electro-magnetic glitch: static caused by lightning, the radiation noise of distant stars penetrating the ionosphere, automobile electrical systems, or refrigerator motors cutting in and out. The only 'noise' that will be heard in an FM system is the noise of the medium itself: exciters, radio-frequency power amplifiers, thermionic noise in transmission cables, the noise floor of the receiver and its audio amplifier. Burtner's project, by foregrounding the 'noise' of a broadcasting system itself, seems merely to reiterate John Cage's point about the impossibility of silence, and its necessary participation as part of all music.

4.15 *Village Football*

Touching the matter of 'ghosts in the machine', Alejandra Salinas and Aeron Bergman, the composers of *Village Football*, found some thirty-year-old audio tapes of domestic conversation and other audio ephemera, and constructed several glitch works from these:

> 'Dust and travel had degraded the quality of the already low-fidelity tapes to a muddy, wonderfully brown sound. We found these recordings incredibly beautiful: their simple, mundane subjects and the degraded sound quality created a disembodied and yet warm, sentimental feeling' (Salinas & Bergman, 2003, p. 84.

Why 'wonderfully' brown? Is this the same snobbery that makes certain people choose antiques over anything modern, because 'old' is better than 'now'? Its ultimate argument is the 'noble savage' doctrine, the fallacy that 'primitive' communities are more natural, more real, more human, than civilised communities. Why 'incredibly beautiful'? This argues an élitist glitch aesthetic of failure and disorder, that perfection is too easy and thus has become 'mundane', that the spotless noise-floor of digital equipment is vacuum, aridity, death. If any tyro composer can create 'perfect' digital music, the élite shall seek refuge in a realm of error and squalor, where 'muddy is wonderful', a yearning for roots which only those of superior aesthetic sensibilities will appreciate.

4.16 *BAG*

> 'BAG is based upon no particular concept but nonetheless incorporates numerous examples of error (both digital and analogue) as a medium in and of itself. We reformat wave data… and then feed text and image files into sound-editing software. In addition to particular sonic textures, unexpected melodies occasionally occur from such processes to then become the 'musical' content of the piece.' (DAT Politics, 2003, p. 84).

What is the definition here of 'error', and of 'melody'? What was the criterion of selection of these elements from among all the output produced by the file-manipulation process that DAT Politics describe? And why is the word *musical* strung up in scare quotes? Do the composers mean 'anything with a recognisable pitch', or 'a series of these that might be seen to take the role of melody'? This recontextualization and sonification process echoes the prime objective of strict serialism, which is to generate musical material that helps a composer avoid any historical influence from key-centred genres. Author William Burroughs employed the same technique in literature, scissoring up newspaper stories in search of fresh textual combinations (Kahn & Whitehead, 1992, p. 413). But the use by DAT Politics of old musical signifiers in this very modern context is significant; electronica still lacks its own analytical lexicon, though Denis Smalley, in his 'Spectromorphology' has suggested a method of both describing and discussing the experience of listening to electroacoustic music (Smalley, 1997).

With respect to serialism and its quest for fresh material, the *Oxford Dictionary of Music* comments:

> 'By the end of the 1960s, many composers renounced serialism as too restrictive; others… questioned its continued necessity because aleatory developments and new sounds available achieve by synthesis the ends of serialism' (*Oxford Dictionary of Music*, second edition, p. 800).

BAG's compositional process echoes John Cage's experiments with *sortilege* (divination by casting lots), using the yarrow stalks of the *I Ching*. There is a hint of the ancient rite of *bibliomancy,* opening a sacred book at random and blindly choosing a passage, to find an answer to a problem. The composer casts outside the limitations of human imagination for inspiration. Only the limitations of choosing – or in other words, artistry – remain.

4.17 Talking the Talk: Modex

Glitch composer Modex (Robert Curulli) describes the compositional process for his work *Replete:*

> 'Everything was made using *Buzz*, and about 6 or 7 drum samples.
>
> The glitchy drums that mutate into a washy soundscape were just granular synthesis using a few of the drum samples, i recorded some parameter movements for the grain length, density etc. The slower more 'industrial' drums were simple drums that i put through distortion and a wave degrader…
>
> As for the melodies, the chords/bass note things were made using a really simple buzz synth, put through a subtle autoglitch effect and more wave degradation.. the higher melody was another really basic synth, through a random filter, and then later in the track the same synth without the filter…

> and then in some parts i played with the tempo… then recorded everything to a wav file and did some additional glitching which is around the middle of the track if i remember correctly..
>
> kinda simple really, well simple compared to how i write my tracks these days.. *replete* was really linear and pretty much one of my first 'glitch workout' tracks, with the exception of the mech beats album, but mech beats was my experimentation with autoglitch and mashing beats into a pulp...' (Robert Curulli, personal communication, 3 December 2004).

Of particular interest here is the use of autoglitch, which is a 'machine' available as an effects extra with the *Buzz* software package. *Buzz* 'machines' simulate effects-processors, those black boxes, rack-mounted in tiers in recording studios, through which an audio signal can be passed, to add reverberation, compression, echo, and other fashionable 'glosses' (like 'chorus', the definitive sound of 1980s pop). Glitch is now packaged and available at the click of an icon, stripped of all sense of danger, as commonplace as the 'surround' settings ('Hall', 'Arena', 'Jazz Club') on a domestic audio amplifier.

> '[autoglitch is] an effect in *buzz*.. its actually called 'rIDMa', i used to use it a lot, basically it cuts up the sound.. it has a few settings:
> cut length: the length to cut the sound for each of the settings
> crossfade %: amount to crossfade between cuts
> repeat %: amount to repeat
> silence %: amount of cuts to mute
> and there's another parameter that… sets how far back in the input memory to source the cuts from, great for mashing up beats
>
> each parameter is random depending on the percentage you set for it, ie if you set repeat to 50%, then it'll repeat the input at random intervals but make sure it's only repeating 50% of the time..
>
> the only reason i dont use it much anymore is because its a bit too random, these days i prefer my glitching to be more structured and controlled..' (Robert Curulli, personal communication, 3 December 2004).

The artist here is demanding some compositional control, at least over the parameters of found-sound 'mashing'.

4.18 Walking the Walk: Plex

Glitch composer Matthew Allen (a.k.a. Plex):

> 'I never consciously sit down to make a song. I often sit down with some a new musical instrument or a new piece of technology and try and 'learn' it. Recording as I go. After a couple of sessions doing this I usually have a minidisk (*sic*) or DAT full of noises (plus I have learned something new, which is most important to me). I will then scour threw (*sic*) the noises cataloguing them (this sounds like a kick drum, this sounds like a snare, this is just crazy sounding). At that point I sequence them. I really

am driven by the process of learning or discovering something new.' (Matthew Allen, Personal communication, 29 July, 2004).

In other words, the materials suggest their use. This compositional approach is the subject of writings by Pierre Schaeffer, and it will be discussed in the next and final Chapter.

CHAPTER FIVE: THE ART OF GLITCH

5.0 Grabbing Glitch

> 'I cannot overemphasize this deal you make with your conscience, which leads you to grab three dozens of objects in order to make noise, with no dramatic justification at all, with no preconceived idea at all, with no hope at all.' (Schaeffer, 1950, p. 32)

> 'To distinguish an element (to hear it in itself for the sake of its texture, its matter, its colour). To repeat it. Repeat the same sonic fragment: there is not an event any more, there is music.' (Schaeffer, 1952, p. 21)

> '… the traditional piece is mentally conceived, symbolically notated, and finally performed. In *musique concrète*, the effects created by different manners of exciting sound-producing bodies, and by electro-acoustic manipulation of recordings of these sounds cannot be *a priori*… the new (or *concrète*) composer can do no better than manufacture his material, experiment with it, and finally put it together.' (Palombini, 1993, p. 16)

These three quotes are seeds for the manifesto of a musical aesthetic whose essence is *improvisation*, music invented 'on the spot', not a realisation of a previous text. Schaeffer grasped the essential aleatory culture of *musique concrète*, of perhaps all electronic music. The materials are created *de novo*, not set out on a palette, not tabulated or prescribed in a handbook of orchestration. Schaeffer went to the *depôt des Batignolles* less to *capture* sounds than to *discover* them, explore the possibilities of a set of familiar urban idiophones.

The materials of *musique concrète* suggest, imply, even direct their own use. They cannot be planned beforehand in the form of a score, as a composer might, for example, hocket a passage across the woodwinds, anticipating a certain timbral effect. It is not, at present, evident that any glitch composer re-uses the same sounds: the genre is heavily influenced by a High Modernist thirst for novelty. The *means* of composing glitch – sampling, sequencing, filtering – are not novel. Cascone may be guilty of a false analogy in declaring glitch music an 'aesthetic of failure' if electroacoustic music continues to roll off the production line with no other change than a little badge-engineering.[1]

5.1 The Limits of Glitch

Cascone further declares, 'The 'post-digital' landscape has become one of multiplicity and behaviour, of data-mining the noise floor for musical information. Like modern day alchemists they are taking the 'residue of randomness' and resurrecting it into new forms of communication' (Cascone, 2000b, p. 91). What 'new forms' is Cascone speaking of? Has

---

[1] Badge engineering: in the automobile industry, labelling identical model vehicles with different names.

music dug down to a figurative rock-bottom, and is now in effect, smelting itself? The Prix Ars Digital Musics jury of 2004 did not hear anything 'new' among its hundreds of entries, which included microsound and data sonification works, and even had this to say about them:

> 'The issue of the transformation of data and its significance is growing in importance, the translation of non-audio information into something we can hear, or the transformation of audio recordings into sounds that bear little resemblance to an original source. The question is: Why?... if data collected from a hurricane ends up sounding like new age music, then its exploitation is both pretentious and tendentious...' (Leopolseder *et al*, 2004, p. 074)

One cannot (yet) carry a notebook to jot down exact sonic themes and phrases, fashioned from individual noises, as ideas for some future work. It would be an extraordinary species of sequencer that could be as handy as a scratch-pad, yet contain samples of all possible sounds. It would be extraordinary software that would, rather than filter, granulate, stretch or in other ways modify existing sounds, *invent* them, like fresh colours within the visible spectrum.

What of the future for such an electronic art as glitch? If the ephemerality of musical works is now acceptable, even expected, then composers will, as the *Prix Ars* judges observed, require fewer craft skills, and little rigour in their training. Education in the history of music, at least of its recordings, might be useful to provide a larder to plunder, a palette to dab at. 'Any sound you can imagine', is Paul Théberge's characterisation of current electronic music (Théberge, 1997). 'If you hear something you'd never expect to hear, that's Techno,' declared DJ Jeff Mills (Barr, 2000, p. 3).

Nonetheless, the art does seem to have limits; indeed, to have reached them already.

> 'The main *avant-garde* strategy in music from Russolo through Cage quite evidently relied on notions of noise and worldly sound as 'extra-musical'. What was outside musical materiality was then progressively brought back into the fold in order to rejuvenate musical practice. This strategy was of course exhausted at the point where no audible sound existed outside music... but for a sound to be 'musicalized' in this strategy, it has to be... stripped of its associative attributes... distant from the contaminating effects of the world' (Kahn & Whitehead, 1992, p. 3).

Glitch may signal a surrender and a retreat from authorial responsibility for music. Chadabe's view (Chadabe, 2000, p. 11) that composers ought to be seeking ways of making music 'interactive', assigning to the listener the choices of selection and arrangement, seems less a move towards audience empowerment than a dereliction by artists of their duty to voyage into the unthought and unthinkable, and report back, freighted with fresh means and modes of aesthetic excitement. Already, there is a move towards this nihilism by some contemporary Japanese electronica artists, who pursue an 'anti-memory' agenda (Loubet, 2000, p. 23). Among such alleged no-author musics are the no-input mixing-board works of Toshimaru Nakamura:

> 'When I played the guitar, 'I' had to play the guitar. But with the mixing board, the machine would play me and the music would play the other two [musicians] and I would be something or maybe nothing… no-input mixing board gives me this equal relationship between the music, including the space, the instrument and me' (Meyer, 2003).

Australian sound-artist Pimmon described a compositional *trouvaille:*[1]

> 'The track 'Depended On [Off]' is a case where after recording a track on a multi-track machine, at a given point, the VU metre started oscillating wildly… some kind of error pulse had been generated (not sure how, I'm not technically minded). I immediately hit record and had a genuine unintentional rhythm with which to work. From there it was a case of letting loose and improvising around this 'found sound'.' Pimmon (Paul Gough).[2]

What seems odd here is that Pimmon's interviewer introduced him not only as a creator of 'minimal/maximal/cracked media/drone/noise/looped/sequenced soundscapes' but also as a 'senior sound engineer working at one of Sydney's popular radio stations'. If Pimmon is a both a senior sound engineer *and* 'not technically minded' what does this tell us about the depth of machine-mastery required of successful glitch/microsound composers, if not of commercial broadcast engineers?

5.2 Neuter Noises

Semiosis is the process whereby organisms give meaning to the contents of the world (the *semiosphere*) around them.[3] Semiosis occurs when an object in the semiosphere becomes a sign, because an interpretant (the organism) has given it meaning. Some aestheticians argue that musical 'signs' cannot refer to any world outside the semiosphere of music itself, so that, for example, a phrase for flute, imitating a bird-call, is not a sign referring to a bird (object), but is merely a musical object among the other musical objects within the work, whose meaning exists only within that work.[4]

Yet, a musical object can at least be recognised by an interpretant as an event in the discourse. So, an 'alien' sound is first perceived and objectified as 'alien'; but if *repeated*,

---

[1] This French word means both 'a lucky find' and 'a brainwave'.
[2] http://www.abc.net.au/arts/adlib/stories/s914650.htm.
[3] Semiotics is the study of signs and the creation of meaning.
[4] The entire issue of *Journal of Aesthetics and Art Criticism* 'New Directions in the Philosophy of Music' LII, 1, (Winter 1994) is a symposium about the proposition that music has no 'external meaning'.

shifts its significance to become a recognised particle. A sonic event is assimilated into the listener's vocabulary of 'understandables', and is no longer an 'object without a sign' but one linked, or at any rate, capable of being linked, with other coherent elements. Its identity is established as 'an object that belongs' in this piece of music.

With glitches thus tamed, what is left to say or do with them? For the art-music composer, it has to be accepted that glitch has degenerated from genre, to mannerism, to ornament; its small message of 'rage against the machine' may have been its only cultural significance. Microsound is the art of the cameo-painter, the *bonsai* gardener, and may also be the natural reaction of artists swamped by globalisation, who wish to draw our attention back to the local, the miniature, the exquisite. It may be a call for deeper listening to the smallest voices, tracing the rhizome's rootlets, its most delicate and fibrous extremities, to the elementals of spiritual nourishment. The prescience of Schaeffer seems vindicated. Russolo wanted to champion, celebrate, to revel in noise: Schaeffer sensed the brutality within *bruits,* the chaos encompassing us, and he set composers the task of defusing the threat of noise, by artistic assimilation:

> '[Schaeffer's] *Etudes de bruit* conjure images of, suggest dread of, repel, signal the coming of, and at the same time diminish what has fallen inexorably upon us since then: the most profound disregard for the human ear ever displayed in all of history. And that is where we are at the end of the 20th century. Our ears are more badly-treated than our consciences, which is saying a lot. Badly treated not by works that are more or less musical, of course, but by the production, the reproduction, and the broadcasting of all sounds that belong, as we are made to believe, to a life that we call modern.
>
> I am gratified that *musique concrète* wanted to be a rampart against this tyranny of sound. Perhaps it failed. At the least, it will have testified to our times... It is fundamental to understand that this music asserted that noise could be at the source of *Études* rather than nervous crises' (Weyergans, 1990).

APPENDIX: 'CARRIERS', AN ESSAY IN RADIOSONIC GLITCH

My album 'Carriers' was both an experiment with 'glitch' or microsound music, and the bounty from fifteen years of short-wave radio listening. The audio material was gathered with communications receivers, by tuning across the entire High Frequency spectrum (from 1.6 MHz to 30 MHz), seeking the odd and beautiful sonorities that haunt the ether: the chatter of data links, the whine of carrier waves, the chuckle and splash of static, the monochrome pipings of Morse, the background hash from stars, and the Babel of voices from broadcasting stations in a host of tongues. Western nations have largely abandoned communication via the High Frequency radio spectrum in favour of the Internet and satellite links; HF radio is still used by emerging nations, many of whom employ antiquated equipment and modes; by amateur operators making experimental transmissions; by defence, aviation, maritime and emergency services; by clandestine and espionage stations. This tumulus of signals makes shortwave radio listening a kind of techno-archaeology; perhaps even electro-anthropology. For the composer of electronic works, today's radio spectrum offers a fat palette of shades, stark and subtle.

In late 2004, looking for fresh sources of material for my electroacoustic works, I recalled the sonorities of shortwave radio, and began once again to explore the high-frequency bands, and gather material. There were new rhythms and timbres, since last I had listened closely, during the early 1980s. Many of these timbres were created by new digital modes, with distinctive and compelling sonic signatures. I have referred to the gathering of radiosonorities as an 'archaeology' (perhaps anthropology) of the airwaves: the high frequency spectrum (1 MHz - 30 MHz) has been largely abandoned by developed nations as a reliable source of long-distance communication, in favour of satellite/Internet links.

This leaves those who choose, or are 'obliged' to use, shortwave, an interesting mix: Broadcasters servicing remote regions e.g. Radio Australia, China. Many RTTY services. News and Information programs from most nations: Voice of America, Radio Bulgaria; Military (strange and aurally engaging modes). Aircraft and maritime navigation beacons and weather services (odd and interesting modes); Yachting, astronomy, radiotelephone services to isolated ocean islands. And many others…

If we consider a carrier, that is, the electromagnetic energy generated and radiated by transmission equipment, as pure medium, and the modulation placed upon these emissions as message, then a question arises: Is there any message, if it cannot be decoded? For example, the carrier was modulated using single sideband, but our receiver has no Beat Frequency Oscillator circuitry? A digital mode was used to encode the data, but we have no software to decrypt it? We are listening to speech or text in a language we do not understand? I consider that such signals become sonic objects, and can thus be the subject of artistic manipulation.

The nine 'chapters' of the *Carriers* radiosonic essay are:

gabble ... (00.05) ... a test transmission on behalf of the composer.
scatter ... (02.28) ... an experiment in using pure 'glitch': static crashes, clicks, crackles, thuds, and unidentified moans.
newfoundlandS ... (02.21) ... on December 11,1901, Guglielmo Marconi, listening intently to a chaos of static at his station in Newfoundland, received the first international short-wave transmissions, sent by spark transmitter from Poldhu, in Cornwall. The message consisted of the repeated letter 'S'... Radio: a new found land.
heterodialectic ... (03.54) ... mixing two frequencies to produce a third frequency is called 'heterodyning'. Mixing two old ideas to produce a fresh idea is called 'Hegelian dialectic.'
BFO ... (03.31) ... a beat frequency oscillator in the receiver provides the second heterodyning frequency, which is added ('tuned') until the signal becomes clear. When tuned to a pure carrier, containing no data, this beat-frequency produces a sine-tone that can be twiddled and 'played' like a musical instrument.
NRV ... (06.55) ... out in mysterious radio-space, lonely beacons tirelessly sing their simple song: in this case, the call-sign NRV. These transmissions are not intended for human ears: machine speaks to machine. What are they saying? They seem to waste their sweetness on the midnight air...
stammer ... (05.30) ... such beacons often speak in an urgent chatter, anxious. driving, relentless.
babel ... (14.17) ... across the spectrum, people are speaking a world of truth and drivel, of tragedy and trivia, urging upon their listeners the joyous and the jejune. Which is which? An essay about the intent and sceptical Australian ear. (*Babel* was selected by the Australian Music Centre as part of Australia's submission to the 2006 ISCM World New Music Festival in Stuttgart.)

babble ... (00.09) ... the chaos of communications: this track is the audio material of '*Babel*', sliced into nine-second segments, then stacked and played back simultaneously. Let nation speak unto nation, let a thousand schools of thought contend...

The tracks that comprise this essay were produced entirely by 'hand'; they were almost 'hand-written'. No sampler, sequencing software, or triggering keyboard was used to 'play' the prepared audio segments; the sounds were sliced up and rearranged in Pro Tools, by means of a mouse. There was a little reverb added at some points, there was some pitch-shifting, but little equalization or other filtering. Software packages like *Sound Hack* and *Cloud Generator* were not used: I wanted the sounds to be as close as possible to the material I'd gathered. Short-wave radio provides quite enough filtering, and adds a considerable element of the aleatory to the audio.

The most 'musical' data modes are radio teletype, which uses FSK (frequency-shift keying) sending a rapid, two-note signal that warbles like a trilling woodwind, sometimes a tritone, or a perhaps minor-sixth apart. Some modes use up to 39 pitch-pairs simultaneously; the resulting 'howl' is another fascinating sonority. The intervals are 'pure': just intonation is the default tuning of machine-measured harmonics.

Other data transmissions are more percussive, especially when one switches across from single to double-sideband reception: in this case, the carrier itself is detected, with no 'pitch' added by the receiver's heterodyning circuits. The resultant chugging, chirping, creaking and tapping rhythms are reminiscent of techno dance-tracks, but their emphasis shifts as subtly as do the accents of a minimalist ostinato.

The use of a single frequency by multiple data transmission services can produce fascinating polyphonic and polyrhythmic complexity.

Short-wave radio is best heard at night, due to increased ionospheric density and consequent deflection (refraction) of electro-magnetic waves. Signals are 'bounced' around the earth's curve, sometimes right back to the transmitting site. Interesting dynamic effects result. 'Fading' is due to the variable nature of the earth's surface and atmosphere - humidity, vegetation, tall structures, large metallic objects (ships, bridges), all absorb or deflect electro-magnetic waves during their journey from transmitter to receiver. This produces a Messiaen-like serialism of volume levels in the signal that arrives.

Recontextualising radiosonorities within a musical narrative can load the original 'carriers' with an additional freight of meaning. This is the familiar trope of data sonification. It leads me to suggest, to composers of electroacoustic works, especially those working within the genre of musique concrète, that the shortwave radio spectrum as a sonic source, can be usefully rediscovered.

In 1997, Paul Théberge published his provocatively titled *Any Sound You Can Imagine* (see Bibliography), describing the current revolution in digital music-making and distribution. It seems to me, as an electroacoustic composer, that one's quest is always to seek any sound that one *cannot* imagine. And perhaps never could?

REFERENCES

Books

Attali, Jacques. (1985). *Noise: the Political Economy of Music.* Translated by Brian Massumi. Minneapolis: University of Minnesota Press.

Barr, Tim. (2000). *Techno: the Rough Guide.* London: Rough Guides.

Barthes, Roland (1977). 'The Death of the Author', in *Image/Music/Text*, trans. Stephen Heath. New York: Hill and Wang.

Bloom, Harold. (1973). *The Anxiety of Influence: a Theory of Poetry.* London: OUP.

Brackett, David. (2002). ' 'Where's It At?': Postmodern Theory and the Contemporary Music Field.' in *Postmodern Music/ Postmodern Thought*, ed. Judy Lochhead and Joseph Auner, 207-231. New York: Routledge.

Croft, Julian. (1988). 'Responses to Modernism, 1915-1965.' in *The Penguin New Literary History of Australia*, ed. Laurie Hergenhan, 409-429. Ringwood, Victoria: Penguin.

Deleuze, Gilles, and Félix Guattari. (1987). *A Thousand Plateaus: Capitalism and Schizophrenia.* Trans. and Foreword by Brian Massumi. Minneapolis: U. of Minnesota Press.

Eshun, Kodwo. (2000). 'Forward to the World.' in Hannes Leopoldseder, Christine Schopf and Christian. Schrenk, eds., 194-201. *Cyberarts 2000*. Wien: Springer.

Gates, Henry Louis. (1988). *The signifying monkey: a theory of Afro-American literary criticism.* New York: Oxford University Press.

Gillies, Malcolm and Clunies Ross, Bruce (Eds). (1999). *Grainger on Music.* Oxford: Oxford University Press.

Jameson, Fredric. (1983). 'Postmodernism and Consumer Society.' in *Postmodern Culture* Ed. Hal Foster, 115-127. London: Pluto Press.

Kahn, D., and Whitehead, G. Eds. (1992). *Wireless Imagination: sound, radio, and the avant-garde.* Cambridge, Massachusetts: The MIT Press.

_____. (1999). *Noise, Water, Meat: a History of Sound in the Arts.* Cambridge, Massachusetts: The MIT Press.

Kivy, Peter. (1993). *The Fine Art of Repetition: essays in the philosophy of music.* Cambridge: Cambridge University Press.

Kostelanetz, Richard. (1987). *Conversing with Cage.* New York: Limelight Editions.

Leopolseder, H., Schopf C. and Stocker, G. eds. (2004). *Prixars Electronica: 2004 CyberArt.* Ostfildern-Ruit: Hatje Catz Verlag.

Lipsitz, George. (1994). *Dangerous Crossroads: Popular Music, Postmodernism, and the Poetics of Place.* London: Verso.

Lyotard, Jean François. (2002). *The postmodern condition: a report on knowledge.* Translation from the French by Geoff Bennington and Brian Massumi, cited in Jonathan D. Kramer, 'The Nature and Origins of Musical Postmodernism.' in *Postmodern Music/Postmodern Thought*, ed. Judy Lochhead and Joseph Auner, 13-26. New York: Routledge.

MacDonald, Malcolm. (1987). *The Master Musicians: Schoenberg.* London: Dent.

MacLeish, K., and MacLeish, V. (1978). *Composers and their World: Stravinsky.* London: Heinemann.

Machlis, J. (1961). *Introduction to Contemporary Music.* New York: Norton.

_____. (1963). *The Enjoyment of Music.* New York: Norton.

Read, Herbert. (1959). *A Concise History of Modern Painting.* London: Thames and Hudson.

Roads, Curtis. (2001). *Microsound.* Cambridge, Massachusetts: MIT.

Slonimsky, N. (1978). *Lexicon Of Musical Invective: Critical Assaults On Composers Since Beethoven's Time.* Seattle: University of Washington Press.

Smalley, Denis. (1992). 'The Listening Imagination: Listening in the Electroacoustic Era.' In *Companion To Contemporary Musical Thought.* ed. John Paynter *et al.* London: Routledge, 520-545.

Théberge, Paul. (1997). *Any Sound You Can Imagine: Making Music/Consuming Technology.* Hanover, NH: University Press of New England.

Toop, D., Monohan, G. and Humon, N. (2004). 'Fulfilling the Means of Sonic Expression.' In *Prixars Electronica: 2004 CyberArts.* ed. Hannes Leopolseder, Christine Schopf and Gerrfied Stocker, eds. 073-081. Ostfildern-Ruit: Hatje Catz Verlag.

Articles in Journals, Magazines and Newspapers

Byrne, David. (2002). 'Machines of Joy: I Have Seen the Future and It Is Squiggly.' *Leonardo Music Journal* 12: 7-10.

Cascone, Kim. (2000a). 'The Aesthetics of Failure: 'Post-Digital' Tendencies in Contemporary Computer Music.' *Computer Music Journal* 24, no. 4: 12-18.

_____. (2000b). 'Data-mining the Noise-floor.' *Computer Music Journal* 24, no. 4: 91.

Chadabe, Joel. (2000). 'Remarks on Computer Music Culture.' *Computer Music Journal* 24, no. 4: 9-11.

Collins, Nicolas. (2003). 'Groove, Pit and Wave.' *Leonardo Music Journal* 13: 1-3.

Corder, Frederic. (1915). 'On the Cult of Wrong Notes.' *Musical Quarterly* 1, no. 3: 381-386.

Dery, Mark. (1988). 'Rap: The Raw Power Of Cheap Tech Crashes Head-On Into Inner-City Defiance And Despair.' *Keyboard* 14: 33-56.

———. (1992). 'Spin Doctors: Turntable Jocks Scratch Street Beats For Metal-Heads, Cerebral Artistes Too Cool To Dance, and The Avant-garde's Hard Corps.' *Keyboard*: 54-69.

Friedl, Reinhold. (2002). 'Some Sadomasochistic Aspects of Musical Pleasure.' *Leonardo Music Journal* 12: 29-30.

Friere, Sergio. (2003). 'Early Musical Impressions from Both Sides of the Loudspeaker.' *Leonardo Music Journal* 13: 67-71.

Goodwin, Andrew. (1988). 'Sample and Hold: pop music in the digital age of reproduction.' *Critical Quarterly* 30 no.: 34-49.

Hamilton, James. (1999). 'Musical Noise.' *British Journal Of Aesthetics* 39, no. 4: 350-363.

Hegarty, Paul. (2002). 'Noise Threshold: Merzbow and the End of Natural Sound.' *Organised Sound* 7 no. 1: 193-200.

Hicks, Michael. (1990). 'John Cage's Studies with Schoenberg.' *American Music* 8, no 2: 134-141.

Hinant, Guy-Marc. (2003) 'TOHU BOHU: Considerations on the nature of noise, in 78 fragments.' *Leonardo Music Journal* 13: 67-71.

James, Carol. (1987). 'Duchamp's Silent Noise/Music for the Deaf.' *Dada/Surrealism* 16: 106-126.

Kahn, Douglas. (2003). 'Christian Marclay's Early Years: An Interview.' *Leonardo Music Journal* 13: 17-21.

Kupper, Thomas. (2002). 'Analog noises: The aura of digital classical music.' *Musik & Asthetik* Vol. 6, no. 24: 68-74.

Korsyn, Kevin. (1991). 'Towards a New Poetics of Musical Influence.' *Music Analysis* 10 no. 1-2: 3-73.

Loubet, Emmanuelle. (2000). 'Laptop Performers, Compact Disc Designers, and No-Beat Techno Artists in Japan: Music from Nowhere.' *Computer Music Journal.* 24 no. 4: 19-32.

Manning, Peter. (2003). 'The Influence of Recording Technologies on the Early Development of Electroacoustic Music.' *Leonardo Music Journal* 13: 5-10.

Monroe, Alexei. (2003). 'Ice on the Circuits/Coldness as Crisis: The Re-subordination of Laptop Sound.' *Contemporary Music Review.* 22: 35-43.

Neill, Ben. (2002). 'Pleasure Beats: Rhythm and the Aesthetics of Current Electronic Music.' *Leonardo Music Journal* 12: 3-6.

Palombini, Carlos. (1993). 'Machine songs. V: Pierre Schaeffer - from research into noises to experimental music.' *Computer Music Journal* 17 No. 3: 14-19.

Rimbaud, Robin. (2003). 'Spirit Trace' *Leonardo Music Journal* 13: 86.

Roden, Steve. (2003). 'OTR' *Leonardo Music Journal* 13: 86.

Rodgers, Tara. (2004). 'On the Process and Aesthetics of Sampling in Electronic Music Production.' *Organised Sound* 8 no. 3: 313-320.

Repp, Bruno. (1996). 'The art of inaccuracy: why pianists' errors are difficult to hear.' *Music Perception: An interdisciplinary journal* Vol. 14, no. 2: 161-183.

Salinas, A., and Bergman A. (2003). 'Village Football'. *Leonardo Music Journal* 13: 84.

Schultze, Holger. (2003). 'Hand-Luggage: For a Generative Theory of Artifacts.' *Leonardo Music Journal* 13: 61-65.

Shapiro, P. (1999). 'The Primer: Turntablism.' *The Wire* 179: 40-45.

_____. (2000). 'Kid606: Glitch Glyphs.' *The Wire* 194: 10-12.

Sherburne, P. (2001). 'Ekkehard Ehlers: glitches and devils.' *The Wire* 212: 12.

_____. (2002). '12k: Between Two Points.' *Organised Sound* 7 no. 1: 171-176.

Smalley, Denis. (1997). 'Spectromorphology: Explaining Sound Shapes.' *Organised Sound* 2 no. 2: 107-126.

Stuart, Caleb. (2003). 'Damaged Sound: Glitching and Skipping Compact Discs in the Audio of Yasunao Tone, Nicolas Collins and Oval.' *Leonardo Music Journal* 13: 47-52.

Thomson, Phil. (2004). 'Atoms and Errors: Towards a History and Aesthetics of Microsound.' *Organised Sound* 9 no. 2: 207-218.

Tone, Yasunao. (2003). 'John Cage and Recording.' *Leonardo Music Journal* 13: 11-15.

Vanhanen, Janne. (2003). 'Virtual Sound: Examining Glitch and Production.' *Contemporary Music Review*. 22: 45-52.

Voorvelt, Martijn. (2000). 'New Sounds, Old Technology.' *Organised Sound* 5 no. 2: 67-73.

Young, Rob. (2000). 'Worship The Glitch: Dirt And Dissonance In Electronic Music.' *The Wire* 190-191: 52-56.

Internet Material

Thesis abstracts retrieved from Digital Dissertations: http://wwwlib.umi.com

Both, Christoph. (1995). 'The influence of concepts of information theory on the birth of electronic music composition: Lejaren A. Hiller and Karlheinz Stockhausen, 1953-1960'. AAT NN08304.

Feurzeig, David Kahn. (1997). 'Making the right mistakes: James P. Johnson, Thelonious Monk, and the trickster aesthetic.' AAT 9804968.

Igarashi, Kenneth. (1997). 'A post-modern analysis of Noise: A musical genre incorporating improvisation and eclecticism'. AAT 9807665.

James, Brett Foster. (1995). 'Awash in white noise: Don DeLillo, Martin Heidegger and technology'. AAT 1374593.

James, Richard Schmidt. (1981). 'Expansion Of Sound Resources In France, 1913 - 1940, And Its Relationship To Electronic Music.' AAT 8116258.

Jones, Steven George. (1987). 'Rock Formation: Popular Music And The Technology Of Sound Recording', AAT 8803080.

Little, William Ganse. (1998). 'Waste processing: Postmodern treatments of the ascetic ideal in American consumer culture (Upton Sinclair, Mark Leyner, Paul Auster, Don DeLillo)'. AAT 9907259.

Von Der Linn, Michael Edward. (1999). 'Degeneration, neoclassicism, and the Weimar-era music of Hindemith, Krenek, and Weill'. AAT 9916927.

Zaki, Mark. (1997). 'Expressive artefacts in electro-acoustic and computer music.' AAT 9707437.

Other Internet Material

Bent, Margaret. (2004) 'Musica ficta, §2: Theory (i) Antecedents, 9th–12th centuries.' *Grove Music Online* ed. L. Macy. Retrieved 28 October 2004 from http://www.grovemusic.com.

Cutler, Chris. (1994). 'Plunderphonia.' Retrieved 6 October, 2004 from http://www.ccutler.com/writing/plunderphonia.html

Hyer, Brian. (2004). 'Tonality: historiography.' *Grove Music Online* ed. L. Macy. Retrieved 28 October 2004 from http://www.grovemusic.com

Kahney, Leander. (2002). 'Whisper the Songs of Silence.' *Wired News* 29 May, 2002. Retrieved 15 November 2004, from http://www.wired.com/news/mac/0,2125,52397,00.html

Meyer, William. (2003). 'Toshimaru Nakamura: sound student'. Retrieved 7 December 2004 from http://furious.com/perfect/toshimarunakamura.html

Oswald, John. (1985). 'Plunderphonics, or Audio Piracy as a Compositional Prerogative.' Retrieved 6 October 2004 from http://www.plunderphonics.com/xhtml/xplunder.html

Russolo, Luigi. (1913). 'Manifesto: the Art of Noises.' Retrieved 1 December 2004 from
http://luigi.russolo.free.fr/arnoise.html
Weyergans, Francois. (1990). 'Pierre Schaeffer'. Retrieved 7 December 2004 from
http://www.digital-music-archives.com

www.ingramcontent.com/pod-product-compliance
Lightning Source LLC
Chambersburg PA
CBHW071415290426
44108CB00014B/1835